THE LONG GAME: POEMS SELECTED AND NEW

THE Long Game

POEMS SELECTED AND NEW
(1979 – 2022)

Grace Cavalieri

THE WORD WORKS
WASHINGTON, D.C.

The Long Game © 2023 Grace Cavalieri

The Word Works
P.O. Box 42164
Washington, D.C. 20015
editor @ wordworksbooks.org
Cover design: Susan Pearce Design
Author photograph: Mike Morgan
Cover photograph: Dan Murano

ISBN: 978-1-944585-56-3
LCCN: 2022947329

Acknowledgments: New Poems

First Frost: "A Green Ghazal"
Lips Literary Magazine: "In Memory of Laura Boss" & "Quelly
            Looks Up from the Ground"
Little Patuxent Review: "The House I Lived In"
Pandemic Journal: "Also There Was a Bent Tree with Ducks Floating
        Past, Unnoticed"
PoetsArtists (podcast): "The Planet" & "Voyage of Bodies"
Washington Writers' Publishing House Writes: "1813 16th Street"

"This Book" was presented at the inauguration of the new Anne
Arundel Library.

Dedicated to my four pillars of light:

Cindy, Colleen, Shelley, Angel

Contents

New Poems

this world of dew
is a world of dew—
and yet . . . and yet
　　　—Issa

The House I Lived In

A Sonnet in 14 lines

1. When you entered, you'd see the red velvet couch in the living room where my Uncle Joey, the alcoholic, soiled the velvet on New Year's Eve, on that particular moment, at midnight. I had to air it on the porch till they could take care of it.

2. En route to the kitchen, after the dining room, you'd see Lenox swans gliding on the table. They held salt and pepper. I dusted the dining room weekly. The Lenox factory was in Trenton. We all had china.

3. The kitchen was floored in a parsimony of color, brown tiles, but the raging yellow walls made up for it. My father cooked scrambled eggs as my mother sometimes had illness.

4. The pantry held wrought iron chairs which were dragged out as needed if the Cunninghams brought extra people without asking.

5. The backyard was easily mowed with its deficit of green, only a patch surrounded by hedges, but I loved the japonica tree and the peonies. It was like we were rich. Maybe we were.

6. The back porch was tempered with white paint and there were buckets of boiling starch you dipped shirts in. That's what we did in those days. Burned our hands. I helped and hung them on the line. Sometimes I ironed them for my father as he was a banker and had to look good. My mother had an open heart and did not feel well but we didn't know the reason then. I indulged her by ironing when she felt bad.

7. There was a cellar door out back which sloped, and we slid down it. They don't have them now but if you opened it there was a washing machine with a wringer and a coal stove with a heap of coal. No fear. Just a warm cellar where cats could have kittens. No stored canned vegetables or anything like that. This was not the country, for God's sake. This was Trenton.

8. I trusted the world then and the Roman Catholic Church although we lived in the Jewish section and did not find out we were Jewish till my father died. My uncle told us. But all my Jewish friends had "finished" basements with bowls of fresh fruit and lightbulbs with flowers in them. I was happy to be suddenly Jewish.

9. Once Jane Rogers gave me a poem in the sixth grade that said "men f**ked their wives with butcher knives." I took it home and my mother called the principal. They changed my seat. I never trusted Jane Rogers again with poetry.

10. Once I was late for school because a girl who lived in an orphanage needed to go in the shoemakers on the way and I was scared to say no. The principal said "no one can make you do anything you do not want to do" as she made us stand in line to go back to class.

11. My cousin came to live with us as her mother died. I loved her so much and made her wake up at two AM to feed the dolls with me. She was three years younger and did everything I said. I loved her. When her father remarried, I thought I did something wrong to lose her. It was terrible.

12. We rode the bus everywhere we wanted for one dollar.

13. Once a man scared my cousin and me by showing us his private part. It was in a park. I grabbed her hand and ran until we met a man with a rake who went after him.

14. All in all, I had a life much like many others but for the dreams I had. Once I fainted in church from ecstasy, but my mother said it was because I hadn't eaten breakfast.

This Book

And the best of all ways
To lengthen our day
Is to steal a few hours from the long night.
    —Thomas Moore

This book is a window into sleep
where all dreams wait to come alive,
where voices in nature live to be heard.

This book began with a wish as the mother
to thought, and thought as father of ideas,
then ideas turning words to make story.

Do you know of any other creation machine
that never stops running, night and day,
as long as we're reading a book?

They asked me about my greatest gift:
the cold moon rising, the hot sun setting on the page,
and this author confiding in you every moment.

Also There Was a Bent Tree with Ducks Floating Past, Unnoticed

How brief it was, alive as in a dream
drawing the days closer
through shadows, not knowing to remind ourselves
that the blur of sun through the lattice was
to become feathered drapes gray from rain.
We couldn't help it.
This is the way time passes moving like music
let loose from a box with no stopping.
We should have expected it, we thought
weeds in a jar would
grow flowers and we went right on
up to the last breath beneath the pale
blue blanket of sky minding our lives just
as if there were more days like this.
The kettle heating.
How could we know we were carrying each other
through time and why did we believe
there was no end to it.

1813 16th Street NW

He asked if I would stay with him forever that summer on 16th Street
the ginkgo trees were yellow with stink on the walk
gunshots were heard often on Swann Street
we lived in the house where May Miller and Owen Dodson once lived
I loved it
we could walk down R Street on Sundays
and drink a pitcher of margaritas
we were young enough to play tennis and rich enough to buy artisan lettuce
the kids were gone
the S 2 bus screeched us awake every morning at dawn
while the man in the alley pissed against our wall
and someone stole the parking place we'd paid $1000 for the police were
tired of coming just for a parking place even though someone also stole
my bathing suit out of the front seat of my car imagine
breaking a window just for a bathing suit but it was always summer
on 16th Street because we'd walk to the press room and have coffee and read
the newspapers
and once to rent out the place we made gazpacho and fed it
to two sailors who were in love and had to go to the Navy Yard
in separate cars every morning and they had a fire in the kitchen
because of fried chicken
but all in all it was wonderful on 16th Street where I ran to work
every day down 16th to Pennsylvania
and then ran around the reflection pool at lunch hour and took showers at
the Justice
Department
he asked if I would stay with him forever that summer we'd lived so many
places
and felt so many things
and I said yes I would.

A Green Ghazal

green grass rises and rises season after season
my husband's heart there season after season

green is the color of my true love's hair
I hear a ticking under the earth season after season

I closed the green hospital curtains and said "Rest"
then "NO! WAIT!" I think of this season after season

when young I lost my gold Bulova watch in the ocean
ticking in green foam season after season

legends are based on these small parts of the voice
how the range of oceans is big and fearless season after season

bushes stay green after azalea blossoms float away
this is graceful of spring before leaving season after season

&

A Haiku from a Ghazal

Grass rises and rises
Season after season
My husband

Take My Imagination

Friend of my mind
take my thoughts where
you cannot
yourself imagine
and try to go inside
coming toward yourself
not through epic narratives
or astronomical equations
but piece by piece
small   fragments
justice or injustice
it doesn't matter
they are just words
we don't have to understand
what we love
don't worry about what is fair or right
please know
I'm just doing my job
expanding myself through you
this is my mission
reminding you who you are
one by one   the vision
wanting our hearts to be free
this is my material
chasing you down
scorching your secret life
asking
what can you hear
this moment?
a poetic performance?
or a cure?
whatever it is
break open and see what's inside
say it out loud
and dare to make it yours.

Yesterday, Illustrated by a Filigree of Words

the night was short
the dark was long

together we made an infinite plan
out of sun transcribed

through laughter and
loss never found in romantic novels

confessions intimate thoughts
implied words private despair

public happiness secrets
and oh how we loved it

all that glitters
is good when it shines

even so he went
to the hospital with no breath

on his tongue and
on the 12th night he died

what is all this about then?
a home theatrical?

a vulgar economy of life
shortened abruptly?

in the morning room
a mourning coat until

it began
commensurate to its music

the long procession to the sea
where ashes are thrown

these are reduced circumstances I thought
(but no one likes a witty woman)

and the weather
served us well

with waves
that lasted to the moon

and the wind carried
the received version of a love well lived.

The Planet

One half a dialogue from another time
here a gesture there a word
we never knew we had a choice
movement ancient as green
now rotted
is it really too late
we didn't mean to poison the rivers
look how the day transverses
light underwater
proving the value of beauty

I suppose
we didn't believe in patience
the Pilgrim's story goes away now
with its fertile future
souls planted by the same river
finally melted with the glacier
the same water which passes from us
goes into the distance
into the state of our souls

Rhetorical death lives in Italian lyrics
Latin narratives in the hands of poets
never did we imagine it here
we never saw the truth of grasses turned brown
just as we forgot the same
river drying in its bank

and the fox to its hole
and yet the bird goes natural to its air
how to reveal motives in these
or a formula for trees with roots
seeking the divine downward
the poem of many minds

sings motion and change
but are words too late for joy
the song assuming time has
no more speech our heads
turned backwards looking on our necks
calling   impact   impact   impact.

Voyage of Bodies

I want to say what I did not know before,
words never said,
a quest of love and devotion,
about people who walk miles together,
where there's green on every side,
where sun's first light moves through the hill—
my true self traveling to the region within.

It is afternoon and I'm not afraid,
my children have left and I'm not young,
the sun is transparent on the window,
my husband is gone, galivant,
he is beautiful and still strong,
there is no sequel—

Once I cried that we were underfoot,
cocoons of ourselves,
merely locked in jars,
where nearby the clocks outlasted us,
where nearby the chains wore themselves.

—only the birds were their own direction—

Motion is the heart for inspiration,
without fear of hardening, loss of sight
or stripped heartbeat—

Motion takes us from the middle
to become the flow, the tides from the moon,
to write this poem,
not for the willful world which needs nothing,
but for its own movement.

In Memory of Laura Boss

When I told her my play in New York was a flop
Laura brought me
a single rose—
I thought it would take less time—
this death thing—
her last visit to me in DC
with my refrigerator in the middle of the living room—
we walked around it—
then I keep thinking about New Jersey
Laura driving five miles to my hotel
which took her one hour
getting lost—
slow and reckless
like our talk—
I put more paint on the canvas—
I thought it would take less time
to dry—
that blue would be enough color—
I planted a seed in her name
and sat on the ground—
It takes so long—
I never knew how bad I was at math
how I miscalculated everything—
my timing so off—
I thought it would take less time to be without her
I moved the sundial to the shade—
I bought a new clock—
she complained she didn't get notice of my anthology
and was very hurt not to be in it until
I replied I'd sent invitations to everyone
and she said oh that letter—
I thought the canvas needed more color—
the ground more water—
there's no telling how long everything takes—
It takes less time or more time than I thought—
I sit by the dirt   I add blue.

Quelly Looks Up from the Ground

(from the Quelly Poems)

Narrator:
I know for a fact Quelly was an artist for she carried paper bags
Around with little jars of paint she'd stolen
This was in case anyone asked "Are you an artist" but no one ever did.

The waitress lives in a room above a garage
She places fruit on the sill for sun-sweet warmth
She imagines she's a guest in a room in a castle but she is not
Every night she visits the mortuary to see her future
Days she sells crescent rolls shaped like
       crescent moons shaped like
       crescent cats curled up
       in her imaginary arm
Isn't there some applause for her lonely life?

Some days she's busy with anatomies wearing people
Some days she's idle with their trappings
She watches the clock
And then the clock watches her
I would defend her if I could but she drinks from her own
Cup of blueberry tea she calls from the window   Help!

Alcestis Reconsiders

*In the Euripides play, Alcestis chose to die to spare her husband's
life but was brought back from the dead by Heracles.*

No longer in love with the dead—
I rise from the slab to expose myself to
the man on our way
to Key West.

Was I really willing to give up
those trips to Denny's? The
scrambled eggs on roadside dishes?

With all due respect to Hades
and exposure to dim lights
I looked up and found

how precious the red
pink and blue were elsewhere,
hydrangea bushes
and buildings with designs.

Excuse me please from the
temples of despair—
I kept the fire lighted in the
holy cauldron, but

I'm back from sacrifice.
The children's toes stuck out
from shoes like straw.

Why deal with dualities
and the appalling underneath—
it's all fiction but my feelings.

I'm going to Happy Hour tonight
in the laciest bra I choose
and first thing in the morning
the kids get new Easter shoes.

Swan Research

[The Word Works, 1979]

Swan research does go on
For all the swans care
Not knowing this
Is best for swans
For to want something
And not get it,
I wouldn't wish this
For a swan
Or anything like a swan...

—GC

Father

When I see the 1900s walk by
      in early frock coat from a former time,
I see you in gray and brown like
      New York, its cold cement,
Small canisters of milk carried
      downstairs by children
Who could not speak the language;
      I hear the chicken freezing
In your yard, let loose so
      you could eat that night.
And of the pack of you,
      squabbling and squawking in the corner,
No regard is given by your
      Queen Mother sitting in the
Chair, embroidering her dream of
      Florence where there were
Stables, the town apartment in
      Venice, the fields to the
North around Pisa, sewing the colors she knew
      on fine silk.

When I think of your father, the professor
      coming home, without money, paid once more
In love and adulation by the crowds,
      in their dialect,
And how he died with pennies on his eyelids,
      the secret note speaking
Of his failures to you, my father, the eldest,
      did you know
Where to go with that pain? How ashamed
      you must be of us;
Your brother's sons are physicians, physicists
      researching the stars,
And he, eighteen months younger than you,
      spared again.

Gertrude Stein Went Forward in Her Car

for Sammy

I never could believe your needs
Driving a Ferrari like a ripped sheet but
How can you think of committing suicide in your
Long black cape and purple gown?
There are hash browns at 4:30 AM
And eggs over easy
The sounds of trucks going West
"Dance Little Lady. Dance Little Man"
On the color TV
Fog
Geese flying over
And we might be written up in *The Baltimore Sun*
The cat is dreaming of sucking. The fish
On the mantle move silently among themselves
Belief and long emotions graft on like limbs
To the same kind of tree. Bite yourself on the arm
Get up!
No one thing works all the time except
For some homemade soup and this partly poisoned apple
I take from your hand.

The Blue Trumpet

for Ahmos Zu-Bolton

Just when I thought
I lived in a land where there was
One kind of every person
Who didn't know where else to go
I found a good luck charm
A flat rock wrapped in
Plain cloth
Hidden in a place where
No one else could see
And I couldn't say where it was hidden
Because I was afraid
I kept it there for nine nights
And on the tenth
I drew a sun sign
And pounding the bark on
The ground with my rock
I wrote A H M O S
Then I made the paper to send this poem
And that's how I meet most of my friends
When I am lonely
I write A H M O S with the light blue inside me
Floating it on the pool which is blue
Inside the clear door at the end of my dream
That's how you know it is good luck
If it spells a name the color of sky
If it opens a door which makes you free to go.

The Afterward Kiss

Insist upon a star which can
    Give light
Choosing it by example;
Spread your skirts, circle
It as if it were the highest
    Point of art
Your mouth open like a note:
    Gently stuttering
    "Give me a vision."

The star may reply, and
    Suppose it does
What if it does (in its
Cold distant light) say:
    "You can't give
What you don't have"
By way of its defense—
    You and I
Will have to create our
    Own visions,

Tragedy, hilarity, life, death,
    One who can dream
Is better than two who can't;
Did you think
There was not
Enough of everything
    To go around?

The Offer of Friendship

If the boy or the girl won't keep so much
As a plant on the premises,
Don't ask them for anything
Because, I tell you, that's what you'll get.
Whether it's a sob or a letter of recommendation,
Don't come crying back here saying
I didn't tell you, because it'll be like
Asking your papa for money. Don't you say
"There was just not enough to give" or "Did
I ask for too little," for as large as you are,
As evil, as well dressed, you'll cool your heels.
They'll sit there, A and B, a potato in each mouth,
Thinking (A) What is a reasonable worry (B) What
Is a legitimate need, while you stand there
Thinking What a Pretty Sight, this offer of
Friendship
Then go find yourself a real common woman or man
Either of which can give
1) Comfort, 2) Directions, or 3) A hanky to wipe
Away your one last eye still leaking and bleeding.

Mama Didn't Allow No Blues or Jazz...

for Lorne Cress

The monkey trap is simply this
A coconut hollowed out
A sweet potato stuck inside

This is how a monkey can be caught
He puts his paw inside
And grabs the food

This makes a fist

You say it's dumb
Determined as hunger
Caught inside a shell like that

You say betrayal comes from just
Such needs as a monkey has

We do not know the source of sanity
How monkeys feel about hunger

But I think it's better when holding on
From not letting go—
I think it's better to let go.

Point in Space

The illustration is of a crossbow killing
Bunches of flowers

Nuns wear black

We stand in white halls vibrating with arrows.

Among the Persimmons

Taking my cue
from the dead
tree limb
outside
with three live leaves
I feel happiness

Creature Comforts

[The Word Works, 1982]

. . . stay out of jail, get what I write,
eat regular, and find a little love...

—Carl Sandburg

The Passersby

It is already ten after eight and
Now they circle with their arms around me
Never touching. Someone offers to be my chauffeur,
Driving backward at ninety miles an hour
On a highway in France.
I prefer coastlines. At home there,
I am grateful for the way the cat
Jumps on the table.
I close each closet door, making sure
The shades are even
Throughout the house. I begin to be alone.

My style will be starting each day
In a different way
As we do our paragraphs
Picking up rocks once impervious to love
Counting them like a dead man's money.

This Is

The September of our loss

The old man who is to die
Takes a nap anyway

I admire that

New York City

I was reading a letter searching for love.
She said What Are You
Looking For on the Page. I said:
Radioactive water, white
And thick where there is
A floating pillow
Carrying with us what we
Are worth
And in whose eyes.
She smiled a smile so sweet
I knew she'd never worked a day in her life,
So happy she ordered
Melancholy for lunch, thinking
It was a vegetable
All melted over with butter.

That night I went out for dinner
And had a small pot of espresso
With lemon rind floating and
A splash of anisette.
You fingered the glass without
Knowing it,
Over and over, casual like
Your elbow on the rail, easy
As a man who never got a rash.
I knew by the shining of your eyes
I'd never get rid of you.
I left control over my life

In a black plastic pillbox
At the Academy of American Poets
Or else I lost control there.
It was a small case big enough
To fit in a purse with two compartments.
You said I had a safety device.
You said you were jealous.

You said I was European.
I strained the pot of the last
Taste of my grandmother's kitchen.
In those days I thought everything everybody
Said was the truth.
I kissed her dog and left.

How To Obtain

It'll happen when you least expect it
Turning on its socket toward you
On its edge through air to meet you
Gleaming when you least think it will happen
When you are lifting your leg like a
Stripper the stocking shining and bright
Something will come your way—right then
When the priest
Puts a small sun on your tongue
When it is high holiday
When the chicken is cut in half
And a green wilderness pops out
You will notice it
You will start seeing it
One day it'll finally
Come to you payment in full
The way we mark our calendars
With different days or
The way we want to share a sound
The publicity subcommittee will reach out
To you before you know it
One morning it seems they won't look at your cooking
And then at night they can't praise your food enough
It'll come to you the way the songs we sing ourselves
Humming under our breath always tell the truth
When the moon goes down
When you're playing crazy eights
When you're telling a friend what you think
Or at the moment right before you call out the police
Or before your worst fear attacks you working
Its buttocks like a brown horse
Before the spoon sinks into the jelly dish
While the sun is still on your sleeve
As the dog moves from under the window
In a flash

In a kiss
In the distance between further and farther
The payoff will come to you saying
Something that cannot be learned
Quick as a twig
Crisp as a two-dollar bill in the jewelry box
Shot through the heart with self-knowledge
Before you can say Bobolink Yellow Warbler
Violet Green Swallow you will know it
You always knew it
The inside person and the outside person
Become the same
Like an immigrant traveling wrinkled and free
You will show them what you need
And tell them what you want
And of dying you will say
"Is this all there is to it"
You'll have known it all the time.

Points In Space

for Robert

How shall we travel together? It is so long.
Proportions are high agreements, swimming freely full,
Passionately felt; these are the sources
Of our poetic conspiracies.
Experience measures the lyric balance,
Fence to gate, hinge to lock, with its
Embodied air.
For my people, our friends, the poets,
Spring was designed without bondage of visions.
There are dreams of children running toward us
Where nothing is dead,
Crowds are elsewhere.
Cities are laid out in feathers of rain
And good sun where
We are building our houses and
Telling the same stories, except for the words.

Bliss

[Hillmunn Roberts Publishing Company, 1986]

We have to make our living and dying important again.
And the living and dying of others. Isn't this what poetry is about?

—Stanley Kunitz

Markings

for Judy

Although the house appears close at hand,
There is a cliff between us
Covered with ice,
              therefore the only
Route is the long way 'round.

In the house are country people,
Visiting on a Saturday night
With new permed hair and
Comfortable dresses.
Who wouldn't like to be among them,
On a simple couch talking
Together, in a slightly formal way, sitting
              carefully upon our chairs?
Yet we must drive long
Roads among towns and surrounding
Villages to get there and, once arrived,
Endure the long way back.

There is no excitement in the house,
No music, no refreshments. But
These are the people who have made their peace,
And after our short time together,
We lose our way in the dark, returning home.

These are the people we wanted to be with
              for an evening
Before their spin to eternity.
This is the night, when later we speak
About loss,
              will be the night
We have lost.

Going South

I love to think of it
Traveling south that time

Thirty years ago
Stopping

A sunlit town
A weekday afternoon

A town so small
Four corners with

Its children
Coming home from school

Green lawns, sweet air
Georgia or

Some other foreign place
Never seen before

No highways then
Bypassing

Sounds
Of people walking, talking

On the street
I couldn't believe my eyes

Three o'clock far away
My shoulders, a pink halter

No one dead
My mother, father, sister still alive

Nothing much to worry me
But the road

Ahead
Flowers, soft aromas

Strange trees
And a restaurant

I see just where we sat
That corner over there

The smell and feel of honey
But most of all warm sun

Beside a road
By a car headed south

Flavors of a southern town
Years ago, my first time down.

Requiem Mass

for Devy (1942-1984)

The Rabbi said she was loved:
"She did with it what she could"

When I wrote Maggie
That Devy finally did it
Maggie thought I meant
"Got married"
She finally got married

I was asked to sit down
On the sofa but
No one made room for me
So I looked the other way
I should never
Even for a moment
Have looked the other way
Just once—I wish that
Just once—I could
Leave something to chance

Devy, did you know I'd
Run home from work
When I heard the news
Did you think I could run
From Eleventh and Pennsylvania
To Sixteenth and Swann
Without stopping

Did you think I could
Run that far

Finally home I couldn't
Figure out
Which glass to use
I settled on plastic

The largest monolith known
To man is in Baalbek
Not this pyramid of tears
Which won't dissolve—not
Since Judy's death
Not since Greg's

It was 11:00 PM
December 31, 1984
The Pointer Sisters
On the radio singing
"Going Down Slow"
Waking in pain I
Tasted the loss thick
In my throat, the
Loss passing
Through my body
On its way from
Baltimore

When the call came
What did you
Think I'd do
You must have
Given it some thought
I ran home from work
On a broken toe
Passing up our mailbox

That's what I did
When the call came

I looked in my left eye
To see if you were there
Hiding out
Waiting

Then to West Virginia
To feed the birds. "We
Do what we can" someone said

I watered the plants and
Flowers again
Just in case. I pulled
Two spoons
Out of the drawer and placed
One on top of the other

SHE JES' CATCHHOLD OF US
SOMEKINDA WAY
Sterling Brown said of Ma Rainey

While running
It is the moment
Your foot is off the
Ground that counts
I use the stairs
Not the escalator
I buy flowers called
"Sterling Stars"
I am featured at your
Funeral
Where you are waiting
Where you are waiting for me
Waiting in the wings.

Upon Dreaming a Proposition That All Truth Is a Conversion from Negative to Positive

This may not sound like
Much to you
Who know Coleridge's waking
To write the secret of the
Universe only to find
In the morning that his scribbles
Said the world smelled like oil,
But my theorem is different,
As if touched by God, I,
At night,
Saw that all that
Which exists comes through a
Transmutation
From dark, and can you name one
Principle to which this does not
Somehow apply? Say, for instance,
"All people are good," a
Result from the contrast
With "bad," no, I take that back,
Scratch it,
We're stuck with dualistic thought
And logic here which is not
At all what I meant to dream.
I saw, I tell you, for one
Moment, what all truth
Was about, as if suddenly I knew the
Specific weight of water and,
Hot with it, rushed to work
To ask if anyone had thought
Of it first.
It reminded me of a piece of silk
I used to love as a child.
And naturally they all
Said yes,
"Streams of people had."
One damn thing after another,

I thought, but I am not talking of
Hegel and others studying
Something as ordinary as
Good and evil,
Dark and light,
Please listen. I am telling
You that something touched
Me while I slept at night
Beyond "a or not a" kind of
Thinking. Beyond that. It was
Told to me
Like a kiss in my sleep
And I am right at this moment
Crying
With the thought of it and how
Happy I was,
Burning with it, waking up on that most
Ordinary summer of my life.

Trenton

[Belle Mead Press, 1990]

Life can only be understood backwards,
But it must be lived forwards.

—Kierkegaard

Moderation

One cigarette a day
is all my father smoked,
no more, no less, and a
single martini taken
before his dinner. You might
say he was the very soul of
moderation.
At eighty, he swallowed
nitroglycerine pills
not to trouble anyone,
first driving to the hospital
to park his car in the lot,
happy that his papers were
lined in order at home, no
inconvenience to family or
neighbors, no stepping over
the body.
I feel that last moment
as a loud sound written
beneath his life,
a bright spectacular moment
somewhat like a whistle,
his heart sounding like a
whistle, blasting high and clear,
a ship just docking from Italy
or a train
at the crossing
where he held my sister's hand
on her way to music lessons,
looking back to me on the porch
in the silence before the whistle.

Senior Prom

Before the return of innocence at the end,
Before I asked how can I go on without you,
Before everything cost more than three dollars,
Before my recipe for dill carrots,
Before I bought them Easter dresses
            but kept dreaming I forgot,
Before running laps around the dining room table,
Before saying where does everything go,
Before the crystal of feeling broke open
            which will not close,
Before my children came spilling out from a wound
            which will not heal,
Before I found I was the past,
Before the long disease set in,
Before my dead grandfather appeared 40 years later
            pale and white to give me life,

One night I wore a gown of blue and white
            in layers and layers,
                  pale blue under pure white,
Before I let go of it all to the sky,
Before I'd say I'm afraid of eternity without you,
Before the waters were rebuked
            and we were calm,
Before the earth was replenished
            with warm rain,
Before being torn between wanting to change
            and not wanting to hurt you,
Before the spiritual hydraulic lifted me from danger,
Before my left eye, left breast, left ankle broke off,
Before my heart was left beating on the sidewalk,
Before I disappointed everyone I knew,
Before I tried to make everyone in the world happy,
We danced the slow dance together with
            "Good Night Sweetheart" coming from the speakers,
And time and fevers do not burn this away.

The Secret Jew

Grandfather,
among the Italians, you were a scholar and a Jew—
how is it we were never told your secret life
at Pisa, a PhD before your time, secret wealth,
lumber in Trieste—

only an uncle to raise you,
this must be why a woman caught your eye and
hunger overcame you.
When your moon was lighted by the sun of a
Catholic, your family said Kaddish for their loss,

you came to America, penniless
with a blue-eyed wife and seven children to find
this country wanted nothing from you—
a literary man who couldn't even build a subway—
Why'd You Come? they asked,

but what matters more is your son, my father, who
thought your disinheritance a family shame and never
spoke your name as Jew, so we never knew, thinking
you an old Italian who couldn't use his hands.

Finding out now who you were,
I dedicate this poem to you, old Jew,
who gave up land for love.
They say everyone writes for just one person.
I will write for you.

No more ecstasies for me and visionary dreams of sleep,
I will THINK my way toward death—
then wild with centuries of success, I will argue with God
and interpret my way into Heaven with the best of them,

I hope to find you, old man, with the riches of Italy you
left behind, with my father
at your side, and Giudita, your bride,
doing what all Jews do,

resting from their wanderings,
reading from their ancient books,
dear silent grandfather, united with your sons
now among the proudest ones.

Nothing of you remains but my song which begins:
"My fellow Jews! I am of Rafael Cavalieri! And before him
other great people, probably smart people, rich people,
rabbis, and lawyers and scholars no doubt—I find I am
with you—suddenly a Jew!"

Every Time We Remember We Bring Someone Back from the Dead

The night in its long fall
brings me from a past—
its colors deepening in me—
particles of places
I cannot recall but which know me
in their certainty.

The shoemaker's shop
comes into focus,
where we should not have gone.
Valerie made me miss school
before I learned
no one can make you do something
you do not want to do.
She made me go—
I didn't say No, We Can't Be Late.
I didn't know how.

       Later they told me
No One Can Make You Do Anything
You Don't Want To Do.
The principal said it
as she made children
stand in line, stop talking, come in from play.

I thought I couldn't say *no*
because you needed me, Valerie.
I thought you couldn't go alone—
and all the sins of the world
may be committed for this very reason—

When I mention a time like this one
about people who needed me,
about Valerie without a mother
and her wanting someone with her,

about her sad face—
there is a melody I hear
from far away.
This is how I know the song is true.

The First

Mrs. Conti was the first
blonde Italian I ever knew
she didn't have any children
she was the first
who had a husband
with a mistress
Mr. Conti was the first man
with money enough
to have a mistress
whiskey money
he bootlegged whiskey once
and now a czar in Trenton
his wife could drive a car
Mrs. Conti was
the first one of our friends
with free time and her own car
she'd visit our house on Thursdays
"Poor Veronica"
my parents would say—poor Veronica
she had purses of every color and size
purses were no problem for Mrs. Conti
she gave me all the old ones
smelling of tobacco and perfume
Veronica was the only woman
I'd ever seen
smoke a cigarette
at least in those days
except in the movies
the black patent leather purse
was my favorite
a gold satin lining
shiny and fine
kept in tissue by my paper dolls
filling the room with a mysterious scent
once I put my Sonja Henie doll inside

she came out covered with smoke
adultery sadness
and lust
beautiful Sonja
her strong muscles
her upraised arms
her tiny sparkling skirts
smooth legs
strong knees
a skater who could cut figures with the angels
a natural blonde
clean and able
a champion
she could drive a car anywhere she wanted
she didn't have to fill her time on Thursdays.

Dates

The silver from my mother's mirror
gleams its stories
toward a light which drops and never breaks.
It says to tell the truth and,

permanently shining, brings forth
an original day bright as this one
where children and other small creatures
played without threat,

but the child's story is never without fear—is it—
and seems to be made of remainders which either
want for love or some relief of it.

In the third grade the pyramids were presented to us
by Miss O'Malley,
so kind she would—
in honor of learning—
give us the key to Egypt
if she could.
Who would like to bring the dates for all to taste?
Who can do this on the lunch hour? she asked.
Naturally I
—who could not imagine how—
said I would—
and, like a child with enough money to spend, ran
home
with only one hour, one hour to ease
my dear mother, who probably had
little money in the house, yet who bravely asked
Shouldn't you buy two packages for the class?
I said *No.*
Love and fear divided in my mind between
an ocean of children
and my mother's troubled face.

"One package is all I need," I lied,
"Someone else will bring the rest."

(Children spend so much time persuading—
no wonder no one believes them.)
Eight dates for twenty children
which would taste so sweet—
Miss O'Malley, always kind, cut the tiny squares
and I kept interrupting, hoping they
wouldn't notice. After all,
there wasn't water in the land of pyramids . . . was
there . . . and
not too many trees,
probably hungry people and small rations there as well.

That day every one of us was a reflection of the other—
the children who ate their portions,
the mother at home worrying about her daughter's gift,
the child thinking about her mother's face
and Miss O'Malley who, kind and earnest,
taught us all about a hardy people in an arid land
who gave what they had and could give nothing more.

Grandmother

for Graziella Zoda

What is the purpose of visits to me twice since you've died?

Downstairs near a wood stove I hear you
in motion, always working,
a long silken dress—
tight sleeves at your wrist, soft above the elbow,
wide top at your shoulder for free movement.

When we were young you didn't visit—
you never baked a cake that I remember
or babysat or held me in your lap,
you were in the men's part of town running a man's business,
calling the world to order,
seven children behind you
raised single-handed in your large house. You were
moving, always moving.

When I kept losing things like my parents, my children, money,
my time in health,
why did you appear in my room with gifts painted
red, yellow, blue,
brilliant-colored toys? What
essential fact did you want me to know,
that the body is the essence of the spirit and so
must be in motion?

Now that I've lost my foothold, my direction, my way,
what is your message, strong spirit,
strong grandmother,
what is the meaning of your dream-present,
a bright clock shaped like a train—
              simply that it moves?

You Can't Start the Spiritual Journey Until You Have a Broken Heart

Take the edge of the past,
not the whole,
just the edge,
the way the art teacher
said You Blink Too Much,
the way the English teacher said
Your Father Must Have Written This—
It's Too Good . . .
This must be why
God started talking to me
in my own voice with
thoughts of
consequences and
ideas I never knew,
in my own voice,
even though I thought
a better one surely
should be found
and certainly could be found—
It sounded at first
like a fiery sun
and a silk moon
spinning through me,
in tongues
and languages
I finally understood,
but fast—so fast—
by the time I got the pen
it was gone.

Trenton High

There were back hall boys
who lined the walls along the building.
They majored in woodshop
if they went to class at all.
I never dated them, no one did,
those back hall boys.
After all, we lived on the other side of town,
in the Jewish section
where people had finished basements
lighted by filaments of flowers
pink and blue inside,
not to speak of
fresh fruit all the time
sitting out in bowls
and children who went to college, wore braces,
and starred in the school play.

I could feel those back hall boys
lean beside me, moving
from the wall when I went by,
then a hand on my back
to walk me to the gym
warm and friendly, I admit,
a hand which knew no fear,
those boys in pink pants
pegged tight at the cuff, like it mattered,
pants with key chains of gold,
boys who played the trumpet
or sang like Dean,
lips so soft—
why wouldn't we turn back toward them when called:
"Hey. I was lookin for ya, but I couldint find ya."
Pompadours were sleek and slick,
hiding knowledge we didn't have
or shouldn't have,
escaping to the front hall in our pleated
plaid skirts, heads held high, too high for them.

The back hall boys were tall and dark and sure.
They'd probably done it a number of times,
with finesse,
not like the honor roll boys
and the science brains who slept
with Holly Fuller, giving her half a sandwich.
No back hall boys would be so crass,
so asymmetrical. They'd be too proud
to take back the other half
even if hungry. After all,
the back hall boys had pink Cadillacs
and walked slow with shoulders that rolled.

On the football field we did
cartwheels especially for them,
but we never said hello,
although we'd know
the grip on the back of our necks
would be felt forever
and is still there. I can feel it
warm and strong, they were looking for me,
and I knew it. The Italian boys,
wild, handsome and wrong,
they were looking for me, but they
couldn't find me.

Birth

From the smoke lying like an umbrella
over the fields
from the line of pine trees along the road
from the acorn-shaped trees of Italy
from the light on the hill

a child is born.

You can feel it . . .
You can see it . . .

Before loosening up into the air
a house is growing for her

Before a house will be boarded up
it is opening for her

The child will never be more
than she was

She will never be less
than in other times

She will be in a different place
from anything ever loved before

Lucky she does not know
what is waiting on the other side

how the earth needs
her protection

how she is to find
something to believe in

Birth was not a gift she wanted

but if it does not go away
in time

like an illness or an ache

she will find
white off the river
enough to see by
and some good to say of it

She will find attachment, amazement
she will be free
to surround herself with her own life.

Thoughtforms

After getting off the bus I saw
the man with the sports page
wake the beggar lady up
on her corner
to give her a dollar bill
without her asking
I told my husband.
"That's what giving is"
he answered.

The Devoted Dead

Everyone we leave,
we dream
leaves us,
until finally we find the dead
have gone nowhere at all,
but like merchants
forget us
when they go home at night.

We like the idea of the dead better than
anything—these spirits relaxing our lives
until they're finally inconsequential, tears all gone
but for the leaves falling right in front of our eyes
while we stand under the eaves.

In this coherent light certain things last,
light knows what to do without worry,
where to put its hands, its feet.

Light lands on my lap
like a pet.
I say this can't be happening,
but it always does.

My mind drifts back to the window
where the ducks paddled,
where the water wasn't too hot or too cold.

Oh that was the day like this,
filling our time while losses damage and rage,

and why I talk of our throats that curve
toward one another or how

I will have come and gone
and you will not have recognized me
                nor I, you.

The Bluebird of Happiness

When they told us of the bluebird
                of happiness
with its rebirth, resurrection,
redemption,
we thought it was about a real bird

because all along we were told
they'd only like something if it
were something else.

They forgot to say that death
is part of a perfection
where nothing exists
but what we take with us,

that we can steal conscious sight
from our unconscious soul,
a large hat with blue feathers
that fits no one else
and no one else can wear.

What trouble we'd be spared,
knowing it can't be taken from us.
I'm talking about the comfort where
you don't wind up in someone else's hat.

With such knowledge,
our surrender is like summer,
floating in its boat.

We leave our sprinkle of blue
in the fields...
But that doesn't mean
we will wait
until it means nothing to us before we go.

Beads

for Abigail Cutter

Just when I thought what I knew wasn't worth knowing,
along comes a gift of beads,
one not asked for, the only gift to get,
handed without embarrassment like an apple or a pear,
beads of silver, quartz and jade, caught from human rivers,
songs falling off a string,
moving from their centers on, these beads of red and blue
enabling each other, emblems earned like trust or love.
Rid of disappointment, here is the gift,
starting with its silver clasp
sealing in icons of our belief, moving round,
angels, stone and coin, gleaming each a different sound
against the throat, capable of heat. Pick them up like myths
or poems. Count them, bubbling tiny
springs or tears, here—a cherry with bright eyes on
either side, a young sun and its middle,
giant stones: perfect, hard, our hope for clarity and light
among the sixty-five. They mediate the present
with the past. They say to trust someone who cares about
the pain we feel—for she is one who, like the lost,
can give us good directions, then wet with memory will
string us beads resolving the hold of our faith
where colors, lost and broken, are laid to rest
on separate stones tucked in upon a necklace.
One by one, the hand that touched these touches mine
and, fingering each to its final end, comes at last upon
security's silver clasp,
which sensibly does its work and sends us on.
The necklace lying in the center of my hand
is lifted to my throat in honor of all the beads I did
and did not give.
Love is the strand through which all passes.
I wear the necklace with its many beads like
every scar on my body, suddenly luminous.

The Harbinger and the Message

We write our words
for those who have no voice,
and those with seven days to live.
For the man without a house,
the houses we have known
are for him.
For the noxious fuel of love gone bad
we frame the tear into
an equality of song.
So that it nourishes
we rain it green.
We talk of green which
will respond to rain.
For the flame,
and those huddled beside it who cannot
describe the heat
or its promise,
our pieces come together into words.
Our words are spoken to the uplifted face,
the mouth
open with its ugliness.
We will write its sound,
the profanity of its suffering.

When the sun falls on the horizon,
lighting the bare wall,
when the dark comes,
when the knapsack is open
for the hungry,
we will tell of it.
From the beginning to the end
we will tell of it.
We will spell out, in our broken way
connected to all we see,
how it felt creating language from another time.

The Returning

I love to think of those
children's books
with stories about
the tiny boat which is
lost
and flows down a stream and
out to sea
finally ending up
in Hong Kong where
another child finds
the bright toy
and plays quite happily
until it is
lost in another river
and winds up again
in the very same bathtub
where it all began
having somehow floated
down the rainspout
to end exactly there.

I love to think of
that returning
however preposterous
when I read your books
and see the places
you have underlined
the words you loved
thoughts
you wanted to remember
starred with red and blue
from farther than Hong Kong
back to me.

Points on the Meridian

Poems: New & Selected

[Vision Library Publications, 1993]

We cannot live one way
and write another...

—GC

Meeting of the Heavenly Ancestors

They love a spectacle, so I wear
a light airy dress,
it is fitting attire
to be in their midst,
yet I feel naked moving
so lightly under my gown,
I hear voices
through the rain
saying nothing of the self is here
but what will yet be written,
they introduce me to the woman
who will be my mother
saying she is so virtuous
she does not have to do good deeds,
she is a supreme animal on earth,
unlike other creatures
who must wash what they find
in order to eat.

Spirit Path

On the streets of New York
I am lost
without phone number or
address of family or friends,
a lost woman at night
with only dollars in her pocket
and bedtime which is forever.

Seeing my bleeding spirit
an angel comes,
wearing my white blouse
like snow, she loves it so,
dancing in the street,
wind blowing, whirling
in my blouse.
How will I get my blouse back
and still be saved?

Palace of Listening

I called on my mother
in the night
tugging her name
like a testament
and she appeared
through the face of a man
sitting on a doorstep.

To let me know
I'd made contact
she turned her head
toward the light
so I could see
tears in her eyes.

Bridge Gate

A magical tree outside
would like to come in this window,
I sit on its branch extended like a cat,
the sill rides the idea like a moment or
a way of giving. The cat in me stares out,
I cannot believe my eyes.

Heart Correspondence

I take the tea,
we place the cups
side by side,
the handles are turned,
mine is on the right,
you put the honey in,
I stir it,
I say *is there enough*,
you add more, a little milk,
no cream, I say *more honey*,
you stir it,
I stir it again,
absentmindedly, like living
twice with this love
which has no need for memory.

Amidst Elegance

Looking out sadly
  under lilac-shaded lids,
    I was changing my clothes
      hoping no one would notice.

The girls going by wore baby doll dresses
  all puffed out at the hips
    while my skirt was straight
      and hung down to my knees.

After all, I was standing in traffic
  but I found a paper flower
    I could pin to my vest.
      There, I hoped that would do it,

Now I could look well dressed.
  Next! To the amusement park
    where the little girl with curls
      slid off the deep wall to the sea.

Everyone just stood there to watch.
  I could see her still moving
    beneath the clear water.
      When I jumped in and saved her,

she put her hands up to her face in gratitude.
  My skirt puffed up on all sides.
    If you join the fancy of the moment,
      it can often affect the fashion industry.

Tarot Card I. The Magician

I wish I could say
he was always with us
among the dark furniture
of childhood, keeping
our mild chances and
half-hearted dreams from thinning.

One could count on him,
strange as Uranus, to
appear at odd places,
declaring immortality
when least expected.

Once I knew him well
in the garden. He told
the shocking truth
that the present
has nothing to do with the past.

As you might expect,
the force of this made
the cat jump from the hedge.

The sliver of his voice
is in our ears,
making the world over
without envy.

When we were little girls—
between lilies
and the bridal wreath—
loving dolls was our industry
and we worked hard
as immigrants at it,

making plates of grass
and rooms of leaves.
He was there, sweetening
the day with its clock of milk,
as he is now, combining
the right amount of whites
and greens, virtue and remembrance.

Tarot Card X: Wheel of Fortune

Alone in my backyard—
My daughters were gone and
even the rain
kept the flowers
from needing me.

The cats
could not be comforted
so they were put outside—

This is why
I sidestepped my own life,
putting on a large scarf
the color of pink and yellow
streaming across the sky,

and I came here to see you,
to share the puzzle
of how love comes to us
unevenly, inescapably,

how it births but does
not sustain us,
found in small places
—the time your mother
did not die—
when you reached up
from a dream, holding
what is floating in the night
above your head,
coming down from the heavens—
that love. Well my breath stops
with the wonder of it.

This gave me a map
of my own time and
brought me here—

My heart strapped
to my back
like a peddler,
a refugee from Poland or Russia,
a peasant singing in the road,

A merchant with something to sell
clanking and calling out
with spoons and cups rattling,

calling: *Here I Am,*
I Am Here
to tell you what I love. Here
I am again,
stumbling down the road
like an old man
complaining of my happiness.

Tarot Card XVIII. The Moon

I see a path
where the stones speak,
where the earth of the heart
is a ground beyond the call of crickets...
The lightning divides the gnarled tree.

Who would want such dirt on their feet
as that beneath the dead branches?

Look behind the burial ground
to the pure cocoon of light.
The tree out the window grows
as your eyes get old.

There she is, playing outside.
You remember her dreaming
the person you always wanted to be.

Migrations

[Vision Library Publications, 1995]

. . . underneath the ice the great swimming was already underway, away, *even before this story began.*

—GC

The Lost Children

It would make a better story
if I said I left
because I was restless
with a new environment calling me away—
I cannot say I was a young mother
on welfare
or a poor immigrant
who was once separated from their tears,
crying at the docks.
Perhaps this is not a tragedy
at all. I didn't put my children
on a railroad car
and then run without looking back,
nor can I say that history
took them in battle—
a political skirmish or
a bank blown up for a
radical cause. No, my children
went the way every child goes who's ever lived
. . . away . . . because that's the only road
there is.
The hand with bones which match
my own looked like no one else's hand
and wore small gloves,
played beneath a new palm tree
in the yard,
feathers, furs, long gowns
holding cups at tiny teas . . .
Now they are artists, women,
mothers themselves, and I don't tell
about bodies held—
slippery and wet—
or the sweat on each forehead
tasted to ease fever
or their faces when I left the room

as if all that's out of sight will not come back.
How did they know,
behind their eyes,
that something lost cannot be found
and for no good reason we can name,
not because of courtroom drama
with cameras flashing
or a speeding river driving us apart
or moving to another country
which is green instead of blue,
but because something far more distant
and prevalent will teach us disconnection
of all we love that's flesh.
I am the one
driving by a house which looks too small
with the tree in front which reaches
to the sky, who
causes the remarks
Did you see that Lady going by . . .
Wonder what she's looking for
where she's been
who she wants
what she thinks she's lost.

Season

Why don't we take what's offered us
and ask for nothing more
even now as I lose
parts of my personality
and the children
who would rather have served themselves
all along
move out from the center
and are gone
while the tree senses its drought
and drops its acorns.

The Red Sweater

Wearing clothes that didn't match
and a blanket over my shoulder revealing
a perfect breast, I was

walking to Pittsburgh with three children
and one stroller.
I was leaving a bar when I saw
that the big tall woman
had on my red sweater.
Oh it's old—
Let her have it—
But no   it isn't fair—
I got my courage up
to tell her, if she'd only look to see...
She'd find she had on my red sweater.

But when I did speak to her,
I found
I was the one wearing red.
Hers after all was pink—
how embarrassing.
She quite rightly was angry
enough to throw darts at me,
but, thank you God, they turned into two yellow birds
with beautiful pale white feathers
which barely stung.
I have always prided myself
on getting along with other women.

Burning the Box

Each year this time we leave a box
to burn our tiny icons—
idols of belief . . .
angel, heart, and coin

Next year I promise
when it's opened
there they'll be inside
laid to rest
but not destroyed
there they will be untouched
alive

Each year this time we start again

First
we lay carefully the velvet smooth
to rest on top
the angel of guilt
It gathers what last
light we see
beneath its lid

And in the center
upright unharmed will be
a symbol most deceiving
a stained and satin heart
still beating

Beside it the coin
of all things wrong
which if we spent
on forgetting
might bring us no more
happiness

Now it's time to close the lid
place the box within its ground
preparing branches
tested for
ability to change
to heat inside
a hole dug deep

A fire that's slow
still works its job
and once again
we go away
and pray for a sweet burning.

The Blue Shirt

And now my daughter had her own baby
and brought him to work,
he was so heavy
he struggled under the blanket.
She could hardly carry him,
I tried to help by lifting him
in my arms,
but he was so heavy,
someone else had to help her.
I had so many papers on the floor,
I kept folding and folding his blue shirt,
but the sleeves would never match,
I finally handed it over,
I never had a son.

Expression

Where is the little girl?
    Sitting on the steps.

What is she doing?
    Holding a cardboard box.

It stands on end. It has
    a tiny golden clasp which can open.

Inside there are small blue hangers
    holding dolls' clothes.

Two drawers beneath it pull out.
    She pulls them and looks inside—

mysterious pieces of fabric,
    dark red velvet, cream satin squares,

blue lace. She stares

for minutes and minutes of pleasure,
    folding, smoothing, touching.

Where does she go?
    She stands and walks into the house.

This is the same house she'll dream
    twenty years later is empty, where

no one is home, where
    there is dark in every room,

and no matter who she calls,
    no one will answer.

What does she feel?
　　Something that has no name.

She will sleep in the silence
　　of that moment—alone on the steps,

walking into the empty house,
　　seeing there is no mother, father, sister.

Maybe there never were.
　　Later the doll's clothes become

Real clothes. There will be real dolls.
　　She will fold soft blankets,

sweet wool, small bonnets, knit booties,
　　pink dresses into the cool, dark drawer.

Heart on a Leash

[Red Dragon Press, 1998]

Find out who you are and do it on purpose.

—Dolly Parton

Stage Makeup

It is where you may not want to go.
It's not what you had in mind,
imagination within hope,
but what will you do with it,
so uncertain the terrain,
the outline of music, with sounds
you have to provide yourself.
My father took me there, to Pigliacci,
the frightening intimacy, the veil
lifting, the feeling of gladness,
or the foul mood—which?—shaking
the land inside us. We went together,
as if we needed to deepen our silence,
as if I could count hats when I got bored,
only ten years old, waiting for it to end,
but music he couldn't guard me against,
sweeping away the differences,
half a century saved in memory.
He took me to the opera, in the
War Memorial Building, downtown
Trenton. He took me to the opera
about a clown. He chose the one he
thought I'd like.

Humankind Cannot Bear Very Much Reality

—T.S. Eliot

All the avatar can do is lead humanity forward.
The rest of us can't wander around India

looking for enlightenment
following the heart on a leash like an animal

waiting for silence,
the powerful sign of bliss.

They say all madness will come up to keep you
from going where you need to advance.

The ordeals go on and on,
the vision ruptures,

revealing the dignity of illusion.

Even this work
is the raw material.

Once You Were Young with Soft Hands

Now showing your age. But once you flew
so high up you could not see the world

showing its grief like old wounds.
Bright light from the moon

made us look like a blue planet.
Night rose like dark water,

a knife edge across the desert in a sharp line.

No "up" or "down" but toward or away from earth,
the sun exploding energy at your back.

Now in your snowsuit plowing, there is a memory
of the sky stoking fires very far away.

Nettie

How to make it up to her?
  She was no

stronger than the wheat
  her father carried

to the altar in Sicily for his penance,
  she was that frail, like the

pale yellow Italian sun,
  others becoming animals as

they grew but she . . . she
  turning into the sky and

the ocean until
  there was finally no place

else she could go.
  I would make her broth

if the dead could drink, bring it in a tin cup.
  I would take the stories out of the

vial of breath I've saved
  in case my own breath should stop.

I'd give it to her if it would help, but
  this is of no use to her now.

I have so little to give up,
  except—maybe—fear, which

exists only for itself.
  Out of the crescent moon,

from these shapes
   I hear my father's voice

calling me again, last night, low and
   filled with a holding heart

I'd never heard before, *Come
   to yourself,* he said,

In all her needs and through
   meanings of her crying,

the only thing left
   is my father's voice

stronger than memory.
   That was always my trouble

in trying to save her, his voice.
   Now I remember her grief,

how she stood by my father's
   chair as he stared angrily

out the window. There she is,
   so slim. She wears a long

silken dress, her hands are like first speech,
   This is progress I think, her sitting still

for it without falling apart—
   he, finally speaking to me.

The dead are just as
   involved as anyone else if you listen closely.

They are here to work it out with the living.

They Live Where Death Never Reaches

There will be someone there waiting.
You will wear a gray silk suit
before it gets ruined in the rain
on North Capitol Street.
You will find a love and be allowed to keep it.
It is good news sliding into light.

We are lying in bed watching
the sunset and talking about how
long we've known each other and
all the homes we've lived in.

The old pain in the chest comes
over me and I can't breathe
knowing one of us will leave
each other first and then
I try not to think about it

and to think of tomorrow when there's
hot tea in bed with sunrise and a
crispy bagel from the oven—just
us two together growing older,
and never dying, the thought
of it keeping me alive.

Driving South to Corpus Christi

for Harriette

I found you couldn't cross the bridge
At Chain-of-Rocks in Mississippi.
Just put your foot down and
drive straight across, you said
to me, a child,
although I couldn't drive a car.
Push the pedal down and just
go straight ahead, you said.
I did,
until the next branch rose, high
and narrow steel where
we stopped and went into a bar
to give the man two dollars
to drive us in our car.

You abandoned your son as an infant
and he abandons you now to old age.
Since you are dying and
taking too long about it
I think I know why we can't go on.
I'm praying with my foot down on the pedal
too far away to hold your hand.
Go ahead and close your eyes and don't look down.
I'll take over now, or I'll go in and get the man.

Pinecrest Rest Haven

[The Word Works, 1998]

. . . love has no need for memory . . .
—Thornton Wilder

In the Pinecrest Rest Home
Mrs. P doesn't know her husband,
Mr. P doesn't know his wife,
but there they sit in the morning sun
waiting to be noticed.
Inwardness is not what God wants
so she adjusts her chair
and moves to where he sits looking at
the center of the rose—examining it for origins.
They introduce themselves, each day,
shy at first, careful so as not to harm.
Leisure and light favor them.
They both like cats.
Both agree it doesn't mean
that's all there is to value. Oh no—
And so the conversation grows. He
picks, from time to time, some petals—
pulls them off. Infidelity is absence
of desire. This, unspoken, but they seem
to know to stay away
from others walking by. The ground shifts
beneath their feet when names are called. It scares them.
Giving up a fixed view, they think of each other at
night while lying on their separate beds. They
wonder about their strange talks, having the same memories.

Tomorrow in the Sun Room, tomorrow, there'll
be so much to do, with that old friend, that old
friend she met just yesterday, Mrs. P thinks.
Not all parties are for young people. Maybe,
she could run a finger up on his hair. It
would feel so good. In the fading side of evening
she didn't look her age, the mirror said. She
couldn't quite think of this mirror's name
and she didn't even know the face it had. When breakfast
was over there would be that nice old man, Mr. P,
who seemed to like her. The reflection said
not from loving but being loved. Where'd they get these mirrors?
She'd carry everything that she had in her drawers
and show him. Then he'd understand who she was.
He was once invisible, he'd told her that, although quite
well brought up, he added. Once he asked
if it'd be all right to open his shirt
and show her he was a person. He thought
it would make him more noticeable
(not especially from loving but being loved.)
He thought she didn't look her age, whatever it was.

Three pieces of paper
lay between them on the card table.
A new game every day with Mr. P. Tell me one quality you like
about me, he said. (I'm entertaining, he hinted. Adventurous, he added.)
Ah, How it all used to be—rufus colored birds far away. On the couch
the twisted purplish lady set crying that her daughter didn't want her,
had gotten tired of her. . . . People said she must have been a
terrible mother to end up like this, alone at Pinecrest, even on
visiting day. Mrs. P added to their list: "You are heroic." He wrote it down.
He loved this game. "You have different voices,
a good quality in a woman." Only two pieces of paper left.
Mrs. P suggested they trigger a good memory
by trying to find their first happy thoughts, before age five. His
was a tiny metal cannon that actually shot match sticks. He'd
play with it in bed and in the yard, day after day—
It was always there, no matter how many times the family moved.
Even though he wasn't in charge of packing. Someone noticed him.

No sadness today. For either of them. If this
is the only self you know, it isn't polite to question it. Mrs. learned
to be more graceful with Mr., not to speak to her old friend
of the Iroquois or how they lost their land. Last time he only
said the soup tasted like brackish water, so apparently he'd
read history at some time. Life should be a certain way but even
the angels feel hurt and pain, she'd been told. Once she said
she'd been bruised by creation by even being born.
He asked her how often will they die. She thought
he had some formed ideas but was never quite
sure what they were. Does he mistake me
for somebody else? Both thought the same question: Was it still
the present or sometime later? Nothing to run after, that
was the trouble. When they sat next to the same window
they felt there was nowhere to go. That they were already there.

BE CAREFUL, Muriel told Coco. When you look
in another direction, that's when you fall. They stood outside Mrs. P's door.
talked loud about her, accusing her of having implants.
By now they should be ruptured,
by anyone's calendar, Coco shouted through the slatted door.
Muriel said big-breasted birds were known to fly high.
Archaeology digs found fossils with big breastbones,
once flew. She saw it on Channel 12. Mrs. P knew they were after Mr. P.
Not allowed to smoke, they still held pencils like cigarettes,
rubbing against him in doorways like bony condors. Coco raised her voice
and said *Some people think their shit is pure white*
like icing on a wedding cake. SOME PEOPLE THINK THEIR TUMORS
ARE PEARLS, Muriel added. Mrs. P swung open the door,
massive and majestic. Hello, Piss. Hello, Vinegar. I'd like to share something
with you. ME! Then she threw Coco's purse over the balcony because
there are worse things to lose than your life, Mrs. P knew.
Muriel suddenly became as eager to please as the three o'clock sun.

We lose more than we find,
Mrs. P told Mr. P. On Thursday, the Ladies' Auxiliary
Aide, Betty, rushed to tell Mrs. that Mr. had pushed Coco
out of the way. An act of love, Mrs. P knew it!
The aide wasn't really an aide, as she had, years ago,
found the pink name tag saying AIDE, put it on, and ever since,
acted like one. Everyone went to her for help. Betty
found Mrs. P in her room, singing into a chrysanthemum
like a microphone. Betty came to say Mr. P
had pushed Coco.
Throughout the afternoon
the body's delicate boat had carried Mrs. P along its river,
hours and hours going by without her in them—
Here comes the Aide ruining everything. However
the news was good. Mr. P, just last night or last week,
had a "talking-to" about how he cut up meat for
every lady in the dining room, so by the time he got to Mrs. P's
—table 17—*her* dinner was cold. He was perplexed.
Only trying to be helpful.
What could possibly make Mrs. P happy?

Mr. P decided to hang a bell outside
his door. When the Mrs. was happy, she'd ring it.
This way he'd know, and in this way they could go on.
She always dropped her silverware
on the floor to get his attention,
but if this had worked,
she wouldn't be so agitated. The Ladies' Aide
said he shouted at Coco "I hate you." But then had turned
and said: "But don't take that personally." See. Cutting up their
meat again. That day Mrs. P went to tell him 'thank you' for
pushing Coco and could he please push Muriel
when it was convenient. There was a crowd outside his door.
Mrs. P quickened, rushing her way through, squeezing and shoving.
He sat up in bed when he heard her voice.
APRIL FOOL! She loved his humor,
pretending to be dead to get on her good side.

Mr. P decided to announce
their engagement. Some people clapped. Some
woke up. The accordion man played "Honey."
("It's funny but it's true," went the words.)
Wouldn't it be fun to have that built into
the grave . . . an automatic song box, so
when someone stepped on the grass, it'd start
playing "...*Loved you from the start, Honey...*
Bless your little heart, Honey...
Everyday would be so sunny, Honey, with you."
He'd do it for her so even if she was underneath
the ground, she'd hear and think of him. And
no one else! He felt young and alive with possibility.

Mr. P used to be important,
had as many as twenty phone calls a day,
a secretary with a dictating machine
and a foot treadle, girls
who were young, and one didn't wear
pants. But she was from Nebraska.
He'd find out what they needed
and give it to them. A nickel for the jukebox,
a ride to the movies. They needed
to be told something nice—He'd tell 'em.
A king is what he was. He sent a
picture nominating himself for
the most valuable community
member—to the Chamber of Commerce—
he didn't get it, but at least he was
nominated. That's the memorable part.
So then what did he have.
He was a contender, that's what, even if no
one else appreciated that. He suddenly was awake
with memory, went inside the men's
room to brush his head with a washcloth,
carried for just such an occasion.
It's not how many days go by; it's how you make the days.
That was the slogan, used to be on his desk in bronze.
You have to know when to hold
and know when to fold—played on the loudspeakers.
BINGO TONIGHT. Spin 'til you win. Always another chance.

If Mr. P didn't need her
to hold the flash cards, he might move to
another room. This would be terrible. Mrs. P decided
to rip up the card with Tuesday so he'd never
learn it, and nurse, exasperated with his jumping
from Monday to Wednesday, would send him back in.
He still couldn't remember Mrs. P, that was the trouble,
even after all the times she taught him cards.
He got bored and tried to rush her, complaining, then,
that she went too fast. Yes, Mrs. P would get rid of Tuesday.
The lessons would go smoother and no matter how much you hurried,
you still couldn't catch up with someone's memory.

When they introduced Chuck to Floor 2,
Coco ran upstairs to tell everyone that a famous man
was coming to live—to occupy poor Dead Louie's room.
Chuck, she said. *They've named a roast after him.*
I saw it once at Foodland. Coco, now,
was all out of breath with the burden of known secrets.
She went from room to room knocking,
announcing the new arrival.
At teatime everyone assembled
to see the man Coco said looked like a roast.
Even the back wing which usually was kept locked
(except for punching 3–7–3)
filed like Ying Ling ducklings off a Hong Kong dock.
The clatter of canes, the clutch of walkers,
the multitudes assembled staring at the new patient,
circling and pointing.
Tall (hardly bent) Chuck nodded,
slowly backing away toward the stairwell,
where he scrambled away holding onto the walls
for his life. A similar spectacle, once, when a distant cousin
of Kate Smith's lead guitarist was said to visit Pinecrest,
causing such a ruckus he never came back.
Chuck Chuck Chuck chanted the residents.
Did the grocery store give you all the money?
Chuck did not come down for dinner that night
or any other, and for all we know
he never left his room again
without wearing sunglasses and a wide-brim hat as disguise.

Mr. P was sent to the opportunity room
because he wouldn't keep his clothes on.
When he entered room 15, he was
yelling that he didn't like things named 15,
and he preferred a little ginger in the situation.
Mrs. P was already there waiting.
She was asked to come
because she wouldn't take her
clothes OFF. It was hard to give her a
shower. The doctor said, "Now is the only
time which exists." She asked if he'd let her talk
about the *now* it used to be. He said no.
She grew more frightened
and held onto her clothes.
She begged, "Can we talk about the *now*
that's going to exist?" He said no. She trembled
with the thought that there was nothing but now.
She didn't want it to damage the past, the future.
Music was put on and a helper would
come in soon to hold their hands.
This meant pill time. Slowly she came
to like the way the light
came off the palm, how Mr. P nodded in his chair,
soft, pink and naked,
how he looked up and winked his drooping eye.
No, it was definitely a call to her, as if he knew who she was.
Sometimes she'd see an angel outside the pane of glass looking in.
She was scared it came to get her new friend, Mr. P.
She looked again and, now, there was nothing outside but the present.

Sit Down, Says Love

[Argonne House Press, 1999]

Nettie and Angelo

She didn't know what marriage
   could possibly mean

or what would happen to her.
   Her mother only said

he was the right one and the
   gown would have a train, white satin

that dripped down seven steps.
   Nettie didn't know Angelo

except by the food he ordered in the family
   restaurant. He always

sat at the first table. She
   always worked the register.

Her parents made his pasta
   fresh for him, every time, their favorite

customer, the one who would marry their
   daughter. How could she

want something she didn't know?
   How could she know

someone she didn't want?
   Her sister Rose would be chaperone,

would go on all the dates and
   that bridesmaid, Rose,

wore the only satin gown
   she'd ever wear.

Lucky Rose—only to care for
    children in Easter and Christmas

while my mother
    who couldn't find what food to cook

or how to dry wet snow suits
    every day would somehow set our table.

Rosie took over at the register
    while customers would come and go,

but Nettie stayed quiet
    and drifted from our kitchen

until the beautiful Nettie couldn't remember
    how to count the change.

Chastity, obedience, silence, poverty—
    broken pieces coming together

to build the house in the sky.
    When you know the heart and look into

its strange surprise,
    why can't we describe it,

or find the evidence for what
    was real, or say what was

illusion, or see whatever pulls the soul
    from the body to live outside itself.

Language Lesson

It was a day much like this,
gray, with drizzle,
my mother took me visiting,
which was a big event—
She didn't drive a car,
seldom went out.
How did we get there?
My father, perhaps, who
worked in a bank nearby.
He must have dropped us
by this large white house
with grand pillars.

I can't imagine why
we were wanted there
but I met a boy my age.
I suppose that was it.
Get the toddlers together,
ready to learn to play.

I assessed the toys
and took my pick,
a brand new trike, and
oh how it went,
as shiny as it looked.
My new playmate ran crying,
filled with envy and
complaint.
Me wants the bike.
Me wants it now.

I stopped. The wheels froze
on the rug as I looked
at my foe. "ME wants the bike?"
I felt the sweet pleasure of

superiority, the first ache
of it, age three.
There would be no contest,
I could play as long as I liked.
I had him by the pronoun.
It was the happiest day of my life.

To His House

I liked the parties best
where my parents' friends
came late at night,
men around the table
playing cards,
women on the sofa, talking—
highballs for everyone,
cold cuts on a platter.
But something always ruined it,
settling like stale smoke
when the jokes were gone.
Mr. Bretell
in his white silk shirt
saying "I'll give it to you
right off my back"—then,
to hoots and hollers
doing just that, taking it off—
right there—to give to my sister.
The sorry part was when I said,
"How about me?"
and him telling me to come
by his house tomorrow
and I'd get one too.
By that time the party
was over.
And with what feelings
did I walk two blocks
to knock on his door,
and with what thoughts
did he stand there,
opening, barely opening,
just enough to shove his shirt
rolled tight like a ball
hard into my arms.

Replacing Loss

for Jan

When our mothers
were children together,
they never knew
you'd wait for me
to be born,
and so you did, when
you were three months
old, I was born to be your
friend, and live just
down the street,
where we played,
and spent a life with dolls,
two little girls
in their backyards,
among the flowers
with their gowns,
until the place
was only in our thoughts
and even then we stayed
returning in our minds
to talk. This all vanished
suddenly last fall,
taking Japonica trees,
the Virgin Mary's statue,
talcum jars filled with
Queen Anne's lace,
library books on
varnished chairs,
hot baloney sandwiches
and schoolyard stairs,
where you waited
as you do now
after a silent winter,
resuming a lifelong
conversation which goes on.

Angelo

If I were to ask what you'd like, it might be to say something kind about you,
Mention something from the past remembered with love.
And so I do. Spaghetti sauce on the bus!
You getting up at dawn to cook it, I carrying the pot
across two states to Princeton, New Jersey
where my professor lived
and where
students met to read their poems
eating the sweet red specialty
lugged up and down stairs under a huge lid.
No one could buy that kind of cooking, at least in those days,
although now of course
there's a restaurant on every corner.
I don't know how I asked you, father, to prepare this dish
or whether in fact you offered it knowing
your meal was rare in American houses.
You remained at home that day while I entertained.
I think you hoped to hear them say how sensitive you were,
a loving father, and so they did, admire you this night, poets
heard by candlelight, a fireplace, stove.
In a different room far away, you most likely wished I'd say
they liked it, Italian food, something different for me to share. Perhaps I
would say good of you. I'll bet you went to bed easily: *this time I've made her
happy.*

You Could Not Say She Was of This Earth

If milk curdled she said fairies did it.
If her face itched

she believed it was the rush of a saint.
Lovely more than anything else

she rose from the cathedral of childhood
vivid in the fields

while the world turned to rust and wheels.
She thought there was love

in objects and with her faith
said "Thank you frying pan.

Thank you table." This would be twenty years
before I'd be born

and she would be my mother who still comes to me
during a certain vibration of song

which I play furtively so no one else can hear.

The Day I Tried To Commit Suicide

I slept under the electric blanket
with the dial up HIGH

before I ate some fried chicken with the skin on
sitting next to someone smoking a cigarette

after I petted a strange dog
instead of flossing my teeth

deciding to eat real ice cream instead of yogurt
on my drive downtown without my bullet-proof vest

to kiss a stranger right on the lips
without washing my hands afterwards.

You Must Sit Down, Says Love, and Taste My Meat: So I Did Sit and Eat

—George Herbert

Even if your coat needs a new lining . . .
even if you have to pretend to be somebody else

to uncover what part is really you,
something will still ignite

humor   kindness   compassion   illumination
enlightenment   silence   true nature.

Well the sun shines without knowing its name,
acting itself out, doesn't it?

But this is an overground experiment
showing we can dissolve ego

in search of the other half of the soul
unafraid of its silence –

How would we know from our scripted lives
in touch with our terrible vulnerability

not to blame others for their perfect love.

Tarot Card 0. The Fool

He was the one
who could not draw horses
so sketched
a tent
saying horses were inside.

He was the one
who claimed he couldn't write
saying his poems
were in his thoughts.

How can we trust the way
a squirrel, so soft,
sounds different
than it looks.

And who would trust the fool
as he juggles
essence and reality,
spirit and truth,
insisting on its wisdom.

Tarot Card III. The Empress

This slender hand of grass—
this slender white hand
this old hand
moving drunkenly
across the page . . .

Passing through this hand
there is a door
a garden you wouldn't have known

where willows grew upward
some days where the river ran blue.

This pen has a face of its own—
it looks like a courtesan
who was merry once

a fool who danced
until she cried.

Now she is the mistress of herself
and her own small story.

Tarot Card VI. The Lovers

Having loved me when I was young
and now when I am not,
you are twice blessed
for giving
a rich person a gift.

In no one else's dream but yours,
I will be the old lady
wearing a white straw hat
with a red satin bow
who says   Thank you.

Florida

Scarred though we are
by what we've left,
will we remember it less
without children,
our car packed full of hope.

We move toward a place with no poets
but there never was a community,
only good people who pulled
praise from our curses
while we sat stupid and crying
that we were still alive.

I have finally let go
of something I never had,
finding the miracle
in forgiving,
that there is nothing to forgive.

Now only Time left to greet us,
the life and death parts,
never tidy but nicely inclusive.
Then off we go again with the
starting up of it,
our nails ribbed with age and
their inevitability.

Should we put a boat in the poem
to get it in the New Yorker
then excuse others
for all we've done to them –
before giving in
to the vanishing dark,
the feeling no language can speak,
the open air of our own music,
the sound of the rain on the wall.

Cuffed Frays
and Other Poems

[Argonne House Press, 2001]

What's, after God, most friendly is the soul in love
To be within her cave.
He's waiting from above.

—Angelus Silesius

Morning Poem

Each of us has a pond. Mine is deep. I sleep beneath
water in a silence so clear
the bloom of desire melts for me,
lightning turns fire to the water of pleasure.

Fish are jumping in my heart,
no, they are real fish dreaming of me,
no it is not a dream, this is a real heart.

Three Days in a Row

Three days in a row without a bad dream—
my luck must be changing,
that's why I wanted you to
identify the strange bird outside, the one
with the call. Yet
it was beyond the hearing of
your ears, once filled with so many jet planes,
resting now in an ocean of quiet.
I can't know these things alone,
I said, It's like language
sleeping, no one else can hear.
No! I can't have it. It's bad enough that death will happen,
but the bird is here now
and so are we. It's not fair to me, or the birds, for that matter.
You lifted your chin, tilting your head slightly:
It's a song sparrow, you said, moving nearer. *I'm sure it's a sparrow.*

Please Accept My Donation

for Ken

I want to thank you for dazzling heaving desserts praising love,
for extravagant birds and clowns.
Please excuse the calamitous leaping over sand, the shouts of fire,
the startling rings. I didn't know.
Oh sure, there were springs exiled, new pipes, other conceptions—
We're only human. Child, girl, man: What's the difference?
Afternoons hasten. That's why I want to say, most of all,
I memorized your paper gardens, drifting stones, the willow trees.
I'll always remember the sun we survived, the vulnerable surfs, waking.
I deeply appreciate the way we addressed each other faithfully,
powdered gold faces, crossing like this, tomorrow in mirrors.
It was all a lovely motion of fleece, feathers on the sea.

Even If You Could Lick All the Words, the Ink Will Never Fade

—*John Yau*

If you can write one good poem,
one you like, well
you can put any two things together and it'll work.

Two bad people can make a good marriage.
You can wear a backless dress to church
and sit in the front pew

or plant two pounds of peas
in a one-acre plot and not worry.

You can tell your sister to go marry the bum;
you have better things to do.

You have written something on your desk that'll stay there.

Carciofi (Artichokes)

for Grandfather, Raphael Cavalieri

One by one things fall away,
everything but the sweet earth itself.
Already this year he has watched the nest's
careful brush of twigs lose a summer song.

He leans his bicycle against the tree. Tuscany
never changes, they say, but the mountains
seem smaller, each season, as he goes north

Toward Pietrasanta. Only *carciofi* remain the same, clustered
to the earth. Year after year, this time, the tough fruit
is left for the last of those who want it.

My grandfather picks them here, although he
is not a farmer, he knows where on the stem
to reach. A scholar who saw the world as
a work of art, he holds them like this,

carries them back to his small apartment
past the piazza, behind the university wall.
Pisa. Can you see the dirt on his hands as he
cups them close, their hard skins,
dusty particles beneath his nails.

What moved him to hunger, and when, that night
we can't know, but he ate *carciofi*, the diary
reveals; a plant flavored with olive oil.
Maybe after the lamp was lit, a tiny flask

of oil was brought out, pressings
from a vat near Granoia. Adding
salt from a bowl, the mineral
makes a fragrance rise, enough to move him to
open this small window and, by luck, hear a nightingale.

Later he will lean over his drawings. But right now he
puts the finished leaves in a bowl. This is the man who
imagined the gas-driven tractor which would
someday ride the fields of uneven ground.

Tonight there is only the vision of a vehicle
in his head, for he feels refreshed after dining.
How strange to rest, brushing his hand across the

linen, smudging it, without thought.

Il paese della meraviglia. He will
visit the farmer again, take from his fields,

But for now the mind feasts on what the eye has
seen, villas with ochre walls, pink terra cotta roofs,
factories with old doors, the ride out of town
pedaling past olive groves, apple trees pinned against

fences, pruned grape vines ready to burst,
covers pulled taut over seeded ground, the sun traveling
to the sea, peaceful snow on the mountains.
Everywhere he looks, the land ready for a new way to harvest.

The New Messiah

He might work at AOL, for all we know
or maybe Giant Foods.
An ordinary guy; it's said He'll
raise the Dead,
and grateful they'll be,
God knows, they've waited long enough.
What will we do with them
Once they're here?
Testaments say not to fear. I won't.
I wonder why we couldn't appreciate
the last Messiah more, yet
I'm all for equal opportunity
and I think there's enough good work to go around.
Did you think the world was full of emptiness?
Oh no, the Dead went nowhere at all.
They're right here waiting
phosphorescent, leaning in
listening, impatient as sin,
footsteps we can barely hear but coming near.
Wind blows over them. Can you imagine the Dead
singing of their pain when they know there's a chance
to rise again? It shifts one's view, yet
what the Messiah will mostly change is
how we are mourning for all those gone,
the grief about the past, the loss, how they loved us,
all that song.

Trimming the Tree

All the presents
we forgot
are here now.

We'll name everything we love:

birds
unafraid
to go unanswered,

the river
flowing
just beyond our sight,

small stars
shining without knowing
what is light,

pencils of sound
where
every soul is written,

each branch
a favorite child,
in a match
no one would make.

Now we'll
point through the dark
to see memory.

What shall we call it?

Athletes of God

The first time I saw my American poems translated
I just stopped and studied
the hieroglyphics on the page,
tiny scribbles of black ink
saying twice
what was said before.
Then I knew
I would not leave this world
without loving some of it . . .
nothing reduced to a single truth . . .
all of one blood,
our words, music and lives coming together.
It was not that the stars had fallen down—
it was more that we didn't need
the lamp which had gone out.

How separate we are in the dark
after the poem is gone.

Children

Do you really think there is anywhere
you can go where they will not leave you?
Any continent that's safe
without old bowls, a half-cracked
pan?
 The tangled wilderness of their
bodies just beyond
 this field of night?

This is not something I went out to find:
the sun in the apron,
the torn pocket with a picture
 of them.

Yet once there was love,
 scarring as red as an open
 pulse.

Can you see them?
Those who faced us? Then walked toward
the distance
 and did not return
although we waited on corners.

Please understand,
they never knew what it was like
without us so of course they
 went to find out.

I studied their leaving
day by day,
 faces like flowers ready
 for winter,
until I could hear them heaving up stairways far away,
perfecting love on their own.

What we prepare for is
the silence after sound,
the cold after fire,
the single moment for when

                          we are spirit.
How will I hold them then?

How will I open the door? And

             in whose heart will I rest?

Today I must really find those things I've lost—

            My grandfather's stickpin,
the single pearl earring.

The treasure box looks strange when empty.
I always think it
should be fuller than it is.
If we give up loss
        what will we have left?

Listen. I can hear them at dinnertime
sounding like nothing ever dies.

The last I saw
they were walking toward me—
time
breaking open into their little forms.

Anna Nicole: Poems

[Goss 183 Publications, 2008]

The only risk is not taking a chance.

—Bob Hicok

Anna's Estate

At the ½ star hotel
the lower lip is painted bigger, to match
her dreams of being a star.
She blessed the lumpy beds, bought her own silk sheets.
This was before the moral issues, the legal issues,
the spirit of the law, the letter of the law,
the causes of death, junkies, drug addicts,
probable criminal cause, bodies exhumed,
frozen sperm, mystery sons,
living in sorrow, wrongful death,
undue influences.
Before the opalescent oceans
where she could never find the truth in things,
where she wanted a photo album so bad,
so she wouldn't die without memories—
one day, standing at the free continental breakfast
dragging her sleeve in the jelly,
someone walked by, touching her waist like a prayer,
like an enfranchisement,
and she was on her way,
in a dress made for someone much smaller,
trusting a stranger because he said,
The Good Lord can't see what happens in Hollywood.

A Tiny Boat Caught Sideways

She wouldn't have described
her companions as enemies of the heart,
that wouldn't be the way she'd say it,
or her grief, she wouldn't
know to hang it out on a
tree and watch it, as poets did.
She would not notice the
peaceful duties of the
birds outside her country place,
the time God was creating for them to nest.
She'd think everything revolved around her,
the way children feel the world, or poets,
but she didn't know the name for poetry.
And when the sun received itself in the morning,
although it was too much to hope for,
she would be distracted for a moment by its warmth
—but just for a time—
then she'd remember that everyone
loved her more than she loved them . . .
Or she loved them more than . . .
until the safety of loneliness reached out to her.
She could never see nature gets
nothing for his efforts, and that
the sun is indifferent to itself. Every day
she woke and spoke to the flat question:
Where is the thrill to being alive?
Even then she lost interest in her own words.

Notes From a Distant Glacier

Interviewer: *Do you want to be someone of worth?*
Or do you want to be famous?
Designer: *If they photograph you nude,*
It's called art.
Critic: *They should project her on the wall, the one WAAY far behind us.*
Trainer: *In life there can only be one winner.*
Mother: *Would you please sit like a normal person?*
Manager: *Take a pill, for God's sake—any pill. Just do it.*
Doctor: *No medicine can make you stop feeling.*
Lawyer: *Don't even think about it, Anna,*
Death doesn't care about you. You owe it to the world to make it pretty.
Director: *Give them heart, give them breast.*
Lover: *Being a blonde beauty doesn't make you a whore, necessarily, but . . .*
Anna looks out the window.
She sees the pink azalea outside. So pretty. That color.
So perfect. It must be fake.

And Even More Than That

Anna was tired of her coloring book,
she took a big fat crayon and wrote SHIT
All over the white wall
Then the pavement outside.
SHIT SHIT SHIT.
She knew now what it was to be a writer.
It felt good, cleaned out.
Maybe she could write a whole book with her red crayon.
That night she went out to dinner with the old man,
he brought his "daughter" along. He held his arm around
the dolly so tight,
Anna tried to pry his fingers off. But it was no use.
Her hunger flapping like a wet towel . . . not his
actions that saddened, but the flat wet hand of grief
against the hot cement of her heart.
That's why she was glad she was now a writer,
insinuating herself upon the world,
having her say.

What Does It Predict

Anna was frightened because she felt happy—Relief!
Was it the doctor? The Ativan? Maybe not.
This was horrible, the feeling
that everything was possible, that
there was help for her, people to help her.
Being happy did not feel right on her form,
like a loose g-string about to fall off.
She covered the mirrors with bedspreads and sheets.
She didn't want to go back
to who she was before,
but if she gave up bad feelings, would she
give up the person she used to be?
And could she afford to lose any more of herself?
She wasn't famous when she was happy.
Maybe this was just crying WOLF
and would not come back again. Maybe
her good feelings were talking about
her as if she weren't there.
Anna wanted to make chicken soup, but
she didn't know how, fear so inscribed on her soul.
She could call her doctor but
men took out their happiness on her,
so who could be trusted with her soup?
Maybe the guy, mowing the lawn?

Showtime

She never fell on the runway, not once, ever,
as big as she was.
They propped her up backstage.
The blind guy did her makeup. He had
a great feel for cheekbones.
The dresser, built like a hummingbird, fluttered
around, pulling and pushing the fabric to her hips.
White satin. What she always dreamed of as a child.
The top up to—but not covering—
her breasts. They would tilt up. Someone took a polishing cloth
and powdered them, then rubbed them hard like
new-shined bumpers on an old car.
Someone else came by
and pressed on the sides of her mammary
glands so the cleavage could
flutter in the light. Ouch.
SMILE! She smiled. She had never had any cavities.
Someone lifted her foot into a large shoe.
The heel was three inches high built up like a knife,
but she never fell, she never fell.
The hairspray got in her coffee, one eyelash drooped a little.
Call Henri! He pulled it off. Call Yvonne! She placed it on.
I LOVE NEW YORK. The music started up.
The curtains, the lights, the crowds outside snickering.
Henri grabbed away her lollipop, green and sticky.
got the freshwipes for her fingers. She loved lime.
Oh My God she had to pee. Not now for Chrissake.
Yvonne lurched forward and pulled the waist down
a bit, the breasts popped up,
glittering with spray sparkles. The nipples were blinking their
eyes beneath the waves. Anna stepped forward,
an Aphrodite who had to pee. SHOWTIME.
She crested the wooden plank onto the runway,
breasting the height of her career.
Someone backstage hissed DON'T BREATHE OUT
JUST BREATHE IN. The breasts are the outcome, they said
everything depends on how they come out.

Unlikely Relationships

Sleeping with the old man made
Anna feel better. It was like
being a little girl when your mother
would make you hug your smelly
aunt for the sake of her happiness.
Anna felt secure here.
Why in the world a blind man insisted
on a blue-eyed blonde she
never questioned.
Once she held her maid's baby
against her chest,
but it felt like a new rug on a dirty floor.
Where did she put that baby?
The old man said she was in
love with her own face and could
not love anything else.
A lie. A dirty lie. There was much
much more about her body she
loved. She loved how it felt
with the baby.

Undressed to Kill

She thought of all the beds she'd known—
How *now* becomes *then*—
the men with broken English,
the porno star
(a special disappointment),
some satisfying   then
unaffectionate references to
the qualities of her mind.
She remembered pillows of dismay,
unappealing bedcovers,
the origins of self-doubt,
incomprehension,
purple sheets,
how many times the clock hall struck,
glimpses of hands hurting her,
the body's study in motion,
pine needles under a night sky,
milky spillage,
facts and shouts, frozen departures,
men: their capacities for worship, then hatred,
lone figures lost as if she didn't matter,
the casually curved insult,
one's self disappearing,
the bridge of mist.

Tell You What

(Bunch of wackos here, says Anna.)
Sex therapy has a sign
on the door,
"There is no tragedy like that of the bedroom"
... Tolstoy
What was the password out of here?
Anna showed the sex therapist a tattoo on
her bottom, a heart, glittering
with an arrow through it.
Aha! the arrow!
Therapist handed her a sex
pamphlet. Anna used her finger to
trace the sentences, moving her mouth, page one,
militantly rejecting the rest. This was
like the time she stood in the spotlight
in the gray silk dress
that hung so straight when she was thin,
and she was on stage and forgot she could
not sing and just moved her lips. Like that.
For some freaking reason
these doctors made you
want to run to a quiet place,
just be alone and look at the sky,
and watch the clouds and colors change
all day long, out the window. When she said that,
Anna saw she finally made the doc happy. *Wackos, all of them.*

Circle of Sanity

She didn't know how she was supposed to feel,
but she was getting out anyway.
Did the world forget who she was since
she was hospitalized? Well, so did she.
The unsanded past milled by her, hours
of talk about her childhood, the rapes.
Before this she'd complained
that she'd pissed in her pants. Now she said peed.
They thought she was getting better, more conventional.
When she got out, she would do good,
then they would say good of her. She'd order Rescinda
to send those three tulle gowns down to Katrina victims,
her old fur coat, and the barely used thong—
Because she'd lost so much weight—
During Celebrity Trials maybe they'd mention this. She'd get
ahold of her PR guy, to make sure this "didn't get out."
It's best to be modest about donations,
maybe he could leak it quietly, letting only the general public know,
only if she remained anonymous, of course, her initials
would be enough. She pulled the scrunchy from her ponytail,
hair flying free.

Toytown

At the edge of thought, a frozen pond melted.
The Guy in armor had taken it all off, and was
sitting on the floor sobbing.
In a never-saw-such-a-thing period she could run...
Tell him she was expected somewhere...or...
someone was waiting... She needed to be alone...
This strapping brute of a man had suddenly
become a minute creature, shaking with shame.
Anna knew she needed imagination,
but trained otherwise from birth,
never had a chance.
She tried to look serious. She tried to look
dignified, but the naked man on the floor
reduced her to simplicity.
Could she name the problem?
Name her darkness?
The side of her sleeve was offered to his runny nose.
Her field of vision blurred,
He told her this was his first day on the job
At **Rent-A- Guy** from "The Pleasure Center"
and he couldn't go through with it.
He was a PhD student working his way through anthropology.
She bent down and took his head in her arms.
Now she could summon all her unused understanding.
There under the bed, she saw her other satin slipper.
Somehow she knew it would fit.

Reveries

Her True Love was in bed with her, still whimpering.
When he quieted, he said,
"Life is ahead of you."
This guy was smart!
Anna Nicole thought no one cared for her, and said so . . .
(Generosity usually showed up as selfishness:
the cook ate the top cut, the chauffeur took her car on dates.)
Anna was talking and talking, she had so
many questions no one ever answered,
people always interrupted her,
now she was interrupting herself.
He said Art is expressing your opinion.
His name was Rushkin. Beautiful. It felt like a stream
rushing down with cousins on it.
Up until now, Anna had been an intruder in life.
She looked into the mirror.
Was she truly herself?
Or was she just losing her eyebrows?
Impossible now to pretend, Anna felt love
in her heart. it felt like a full leaf on an old tree.
Pain could not reach her now,
her wishes no longer starting before her,
she was in bed with a sweet soul, an intellect,
someone she could ask anything.
She took him in her large arms, whispering,
How did the cardinal get so red?

Navy Wife

[Goss 183 Publications, 2010]

He's flying over a postage stamp
Landing on a dime without a light
... The phone rings   a voice says
I know you're alone
I'm watching you ...

—GC

Welcome Aboard: A Service Manual for the Naval Officer's Wife by Florence Ridgely Johnson © 1951 (Pg. 182)

"Within the Continental Limits"

At home you will need something more
than housework to keep you occupied.
If you know how to sew, this is a good opportunity
to make clothes you will need for the next season
without being interrupted to cook lunch
or find a color ornament (sic: for your husband),
and this is a good time to knit or crochet
or do needlepoint,
and an especially good time to catch up
on your correspondence.
You will need some recreation.
Perhaps you might want to study.
If so, work can be combined with pleasure...
take a course in a language,
sewing, weaving, pottery making, bridge.
There is always local sightseeing.
You can take short motor trips
to nearby places of interest.
There are a thousand and one ways
to fill in time enjoyably during his cruise.

Cuban Missile Crisis 1962

My cousin called from New York,
saying we might just lose Florida.

I shouted, Hey I'm right near Orlando. And then I hung up.

Our men were gone.
What sea Ken was on, I did not know, but that he was alerted,
I was sure, probably in his cockpit, ready to launch.

The wives were told to take their children
and go into their hallway, line it with mattresses
and bring two weeks supply of food.

May Day!
I had an 8-year-old and twin 3-year-old girls.

Let's go, I said.

We rushed through the trunk for my
mother's old mink stoles, some Barbie high heels,
skirts torn from gowns.

The other wives had left town, had somewhere to go.
A single tank drove down our empty street in Sanford, Florida, USA.
We followed it under the palm trees, onto the sandy road.

The bright Florida sun roared across our backs.
I said let's play dress-ups. Sparkling skirts and glittering shoes,
necklaces of bright glass beads, bracelets up our arms.

Come on. Now we were ready.
Let's go out with the bomb! Then we'll have lunch.
We'll picnic under the palm.

Casualty Assistance Officer

Whidbey Island, Washington, 1965

The knock on the door was not for me.

The officer in Dress Blues with his hat in his hand,
was the angel of death we never wanted to see.

The knock on the door was not for me.

It was for Carol, the beautiful tan blonde
in the white linen dress,
the one who played tennis and held our hands.

It is her house we are in now,
every one of us
pressed up against it,
making coffee,
taking the children.

Each of us is stunned into motion, trying to fill
the hard planes of separation beyond what one could see.

The knock on the door was not for me.

Welcome Aboard: A Service Manual ©1951 (Pg. 159)

"On Receipt of Orders"

If you can keep the sun off your knees while driving,
shorts are the most comfortable thing to travel in,
but if you wear them out of the car
in some of the small communities
throughout the middle of the country,
you may be looked at askance.
The playsuit with shirt and shorts in one piece
is cool and comfortable and
the extra matching skirt can be spread
over your knees in the car
as a protection against the sun and can be
slipped on when you stop and get out.
A scarf or small cap of some kind
(a golf cap is wonderful)
helps keep the dust out of your hair.
Pack so that you will only have to
open one bag each night
and your husband will bless you.

Wife

When we were young and estranged
we met in the hall. He pressed
me against his uniform, my
satin blouse, we fell to the
floor in love—no we did not—
we stood—I wore my chiffon
blouse, distant in the kitchen—
or we walked in the park—no—
it was our wish that we
fall to the floor in a way
like never before but—no—
it must have been some other selves
who should have worn those clothes.
Now he is sailing away.

Navy Wife

1964
Among things lost was a golden rose hanging on a chain
given by a teacher before
my 5-year-old daughter had her tonsils out.
I vacuumed it up on the rug. I didn't know
how, then, to open the machine. The twins were three years old
drinking bottles, standing on the couch. I was
too pregnant to lean over, to find the chain.
I said we'd try to find another one. I promise,
but I'd have to leave her at the hospital, alone, overnight.

1970
My youngest daughter loved that sweater, the one with the angora animals.
She got it for Christmas, it was thrown in the wash by accident,
a gift from her Nana, tiny fuzzy creatures shrunk beyond wearing.
So much was hurried. We tried to find one like it.

1944
The sweater was cut off my arm when I broke the bone.
Roosters knitted on the wool, a figured sweater, the first of its kind,
such a generous grandmother to give such a present. I walked in front
of a car. I was told to tell the insurance company
it was not my fault. The only sweater we found to replace it was
blue with white stars and that was four years later.

1950
The gold Bulova watch I wanted so much, waiting for so long, I finally
got for high school graduation. What made me go running into the ocean,
the next day, swimming, without taking it off.

1964

My husband lost his friends. He says he cannot count them,
he cannot see their faces. He cannot say their names.
He felt their presence, flying on his wing, protecting him. He cared so much.

1962

The crystal earring brought back from a war cruise
was thrown out with the purse.
The present, bought on shore duty, a single day off the carrier,
a jewel still warm in my hand. The only one left.

The Magellanic Clouds of Viet Nam

How far we travelled, sweetheart...

—Stephen Spender

When you came home from
the minutes of war
sick from passion and duty

you lived
in the past

and the future

anywhere but here.

You walked in
suspicious

of desires and
other rites of loss.

"Promise me you'll
only dream
dreams of me," I'd said

but that spoke to a life
where death
had not yet reached

and a time
smaller
than your experience.

It took eleven years
of walking
for you to reach
the marble names

afraid you'd find yours
on the list
and afraid you wouldn't.

Fated to be alive
when your friends were dead

you smoothed
your mournful clothes
and turned toward the Memorial.

I found Buzz Eidsmoe's name
you called. *This is why I was*
afraid to come
afraid to see it.
It's here. I see it.
I can remember their faces
but not all their names.

You talked about perspective
the marble of memorial.

The angles
simple
unadorned

contained by a sun

shining on black surfaces

surprisingly radiant.

Welcome Aboard: A Service Manual ©1951 (Pg. 103)

"Naval Social Usage"

So here are what might be called the rules for a Visit:

1. Being completely informal, as opposed to the "Call,"
is paid to a neighbor or friend whom you know very well.
2. A Visit, as such, is never paid to a stranger or acquaintance.
3. A Visit may be paid at any time of day or early evening that
is convenient to the host.
4. Arrangements may be made ahead by telephone for a Visit.
5. You may wear whatever is suitable.
6. You may stay as long as you feel welcome.

Stateside

From the white winters
from the stone letters
after guarding the night
the end of our differences
from the colonized heart
the mournful moral lessons
into the electronic age
the versions of ourselves
in the breeze from the waters
hoarding its memories.

Sounds Like Something I Would Say

[Goss 183 Publications, 2010]

*All you love of her
lies here...*

—Edna St. Vincent Millay

Other People's Arms

What is this illegal operation
        I've performed while
Watching from a distance?
Age! What a surprise!
Leaving us in the dark,
        Reaching—
I brush your hand against mine,
I meet your gaze,
We look out different windows
        To see the same tree.
All days come to this, pears
        Turning to wine, bucketing
        Up and down
Against shafting memory.

Say What You Will

I miss them. The women of the 1950s, plain sheath dresses, large plastic earrings, coiffed hair. How they moved in the room. The one with misshapen legs would be complimented for her stockings. The women greet each other and touch hands. I lean back against the white linen lady, my back against her heart. She places her hand over my shoulder high on my chest and holds me to her. It says I know something bad, I will never tell you. Your husband. There is no redress. How I miss them, the women of the 60s, sandals and long colorful skirts, flopping their brilliance for sale. A high level of amiability, motives for manners, the women of the 80s clicking high heels at meetings, lunch, umbrellas lost in restaurants. They do not like the light, these spirits. I lean back. I can still feel her hand on my chest, they died just when everything was going so well, and she almost a perfect stranger.

Equipoise

for Robert Sargent

Today I tripped and dropped the cake
           outside your window
spreading the grass with whipped cream for sparrows to eat.

My hands were emptied of pleasure, but
           I went inside. You were
dressed for company, a bright blue shirt to match your eyes.

"She's here" the helper shouts and your blind eyes see,
           just as, almost deaf,
you can always hear me.

Today I tell you to go on with your writing.
           although 94 and knocked back by stroke,
I ask your "process." Poetry, you say. "But how can you write?"

You say you hold a pencil, do a line, then have it read back to you.
           You think you can manage.
"Family secrets," I whisper. A good idea for a poem.

I lean in as we do every week over lunch.
           I repeat the story you told me 30 years ago.
You lowered your voice then to tell me how your mother was found

sleeping with your uncle. Today I make you enter
           the house of memory,
"And who found her?" I ask.

Winifred, my little sister.
I wanted to know who else was told, what your mother said,
           why your mother's other sister helped her out,
loaned a room in the house. Adultery. We talk about adultery,

how you put false information in your journal for your wife to find.
           Your eyes are cloudy
yet you look straight in my face. It says we've been through a lot,

stories told each other over the years, our friendship a fragile line,
we walked and never fell off.
Once I said you did not express enough appreciation.

Today I say, "I love you," and you say, "Thank you. Thank you."
You say it five times in one hour.
The line sweeps back, holds us in, correcting its curves.

There is nothing we do not know. I avoid painful subjects.
I close the door,
stepping over the sweet confection melting in the sun.

Crystal Radio

The little boys are playing in the workshop.
The monologue is of screwdrivers
and broken radios. They lean over
wires, untying commandments of mystery.
The plain boxes disassembled,
a grandfather pulls apart all
colors. Love makes no sound
while Newton's
laws of motion are at work,
speeding between the tongue and the mind.
They speak. They make motion from parts.
They create what I have never written.
They don't know this can't go on without them.
They don't know what a memory is worth.
It is a sight to command, the
old man leaning over, the boys in a dream
of their own making. He is saying
"I'm not done with you yet."
They are thinking this will go on forever.

This Sounds Like Something I Would Say

What I did, more than likely, when we stood up, in that movie
theater, was swallow. That day, at age thirteen, love was given to me.
Today, clouds look like they did,
small bunches, white puffs, behind branches.
Later, he would swear he never heard me gulp, although
I held saliva in my mouth for two hours, because the body,
even just a throat, should not make noise at age 13.
Today, on a day just like this, Jan and I would walk down the Hill.
Jan is with me in kindergarten, and everything smells like bread.
We are sitting together on small chairs at the Hermitage Library.
That was before we knew what Eve really did. Even then we
wondered about the stories, the room we were in: Did the
light make the path to the door?
Or did the path make the light? There was no one to ask
about bright windows, shadows, or what Eve would do
and what was already widening within us.

Tomato Pies, 25 Cents

Tomato pies are what we called them, those days,
before pizza came in,
at my grandmother's restaurant
in Trenton New Jersey.
My grandfather is rolling meatballs
in the back. He studied to be a priest in Sicily but
saved his sister Maggie from marrying a bad guy
by coming to America.
Uncle Joey is rolling dough and spooning sauce.
Uncle Joey is scrubbed clean,
sobered up, in a white starched shirt, after
cops delivered him home just hours before.
The waitresses are helping
themselves to handfuls of cash out of the drawer,
playing the numbers with Moon Mullin
and Shad, sent in from Broad Street. 1942,
tomato pies with cheese, 25 cents.
With anchovies, large, 50 cents.
A whole dinner is 60 cents (before 6:00 PM).
How the soldiers, bussed in from Fort Dix,
would stand outside all the way down Warren Street,
waiting for this new taste treat,
young guys in uniform,
lined up and laughing, learning Italian
before being shipped out to fight the last great war.

Sally Dies

for Sally Trebbe, June, 2008

There goes my past again   the mind worn as thin as   this
summer dress   There goes Sally   like the rain against the
wall   slighter now   leaving   so sweet   like   something to
celebrate   together   days so sweet   like   sunny cupcakes
being young   I mean   I will make a mistake saying this
but I was talking about   pressing five children   into a car   to
go to the bad   section   to buy fabrics   under   a lemony
sky   before it turned gray   This is   so ordinary
forgive me   the Japanese   dinners   we cooked   and
babies vomited   forgive me   I cannot seem   to   do
better   being with her   the whole of it   I realize   in
poetry   we cannot   say we were young   but the arms
our arms   held   so much   that   moved
(the tail   of the bird that just went by)   outside   now   (a
tangle of trees)   I was talking about these hands   our hands
that made so much   of color   and food   these hands   the
same ones   mine   reach   into a temple of   words   to pull
out   some breath   of someone   once condensed   now
the breath of words   well that makes it harder   telling
how we became   women   in soft wool suits   and high
heels   and umbrellas   rushing in   restaurants   in
Washington   a lawyer   and a producer   extravagantly
available   shamelessly   big   with   love   for each other
when it could   have been   otherwise   I will make a
mistake saying this   but there goes   Sally   with her
laugh   and that   makes it all the harder   to remind you
when the day sheds itself   of Sally   and her box of paints
and flowers   let it not be forgotten   there is   someone left
one of us   is always left.

The Old Woman in the Bed

Listening is how we learn to speak said
    the old woman in the bed.
Does the moon know it means the end of the day?
She asks Nurse's footsteps as they walk away.

Leaves outside rattle like
    gold earrings? Left in what black jacket?
In what closet? How many times has she lost them?
The old lady lying in bed seems, to others, merely

a body like cloth, wind blowing over her life,
    a blanket, with legs flung out.
The future is a mother of roads moving ahead
calling her blood to follow. She listens.

There goes the self again, in the nurse's pocket.
    Between mind and thought, the
moon in autumn catches the curtain,
a candling light dimming her day.

She thinks she hears voices crying like crickets,
    never mind, she will pretend today
was her choice, cradling sorrow like love.
Tubes in her veins are to make her beautiful,

She's a girl shining on top of a star.
    There is good everywhere, even
the medicine feels good, a cool hand against
the hot foaming of her heart. Even Judas was good

if he made Jesus rise again.
    In Italy there were hunters who chased rabbits,
they found pinecones, on hills acrid with grapes,
they went for chestnuts after the rain, and snails,

yes the snails. Once she saw crops turn
    to smoke in the fields.
Once she saw morning come. Now she
Sees it again, but dimmer.

She wipes crumbs from the table of her childhood.
    Putting things back, that's all death is.
Now she feels September through the window,
a red fox who will take apples from her hand.

The day falls outside her like another question.
    Everything is still alive—
her mother in the kitchen cooking—
someone playing the piano, it sounds like

yellow trees, and yellow bushes where a yellow cat
    lies in a yellow hedge. Even the silence in dreams
vanishes, no complaints because the
listening has always been fine. It is how we learn to speak.

Take that train whistle in the distance,
    the truth that sings back is a sound that
needs nothing from her. She wonders where it's been,
where it's headed, why it's going home without her.

Time Travel

My father was the brightest, most promising
young man at the bank,
or so he was told—smart, articulate,
good with numbers, kind to the
customers, drawing in Italians from
the neighborhood. He read their
letters from the Old Country, planned
savings so sons could go to college.

He was the best there was, that must
be why the President called him in
his large office, offering an unexpected
prize—to be an officer
of The Banking Company. How
good my father must have felt. Was he
flushed with surprise? excited?
"However," the head man
said, "you'll have to change
your last name. You understand. A bank
Officer is different from an ordinary Teller."

What was his first thought? What scenes did he
see? His own father, Rafael, in Pisa,
at the University? The young agronomist
leaning over his drawings of a
gas-driven tractor designed to harvest
the vineyards? What did he remember
of the Piazza dei Cavalieri—or of the

company which took the patent away without
credit or cash, or Rafael in this new country,
with a final note to his children of his failures.
How many moments did it take
before my father refused the
offer? Did he look at the clock on
the wall, move his feet on the
carpet, turning slowly to the door?

Twenty years later, he
obtained the desk after all,
nearly one hundred years away
from Pisa and then California, harvesting
its grapes with a stolen gas-driven
engine, common machinery, now. All things
moving slowly, just a matter of time.

Silence, the Way It Hides the Truth

Silence, you wanderer, with your purposeful imagery—
nothing inflames the past as much as you do.

How many places can you lead the mind at once—
Perception? (Oh, now you look down)—invention?
(Now you nod)—so much you hold, to darkness,
then to bliss.
Look at this collection of poems—most expressive,
don't you think? Various patterns fused together? All
with Silence. So, how many
different directions do you own, replenished by words?
You surround language with sensuality as if you were alive.
You want to do us in,
your careless spirit, avoiding my gaze,
taking us down the road with you.
Silence, the mother of all muses,
always the winner, in wait for us, with your cunning,
treating me to the final word.

Epithalamion

for Avideh Shashaani

The first heart is made of self,
A spirit you brought with you and that
Stays after you leave.

The other is flesh and blood of
The stranger you always wanted to know.

But the heart I love best is where
The two hearts meet, overlap,
Forming a tiny center.

This is the place from which all things
Begin and to which all things return,

A heartbeat that can be heard.
If you cannot listen, who will?
And if you can find safety in fear,

Within the sound of this wilderness,
There may be nothing outside you will need.

Here Is a Poem You Can Hide In

When you come to wherever
failed hopes go, turn
here instead,
where my child's voice is heard
in the night, still damp from dreams.

Talk of sweet surrender against the
February snow, and then turn inward,
where silver trims the bitter limbs.

I'm not afraid to mention
precious aspirations and
all we know went wrong,

I'm here with you,
under the same sun and same moon,
above darkness,
right here, the source of prayer,
right here in my hand.

Millie's Sunshine Tiki Villas

A Novella in Verse

[Goss 183 Publications, 2011]

...A lot less lungs and much less wind
But ain't I lucky I can still breathe in.
—Maya Angelou

Coco lived in bungalow Number One and it was a good thing
she was nine away from Number Ten, away from Muriel,
for try as they did, no good came from their conversations.
In Unit I and Unit 10 lights burned late into the night,
where it's rumored each was writing competing memoirs
to see who could finish first. Neither had done much but marry,
have tea at four and bury a husband. But literature being what it is,
much could be made of it. We can only imagine how anxiously
the monographs were awaited by fellow residents, anxious for a look
inward. What a strange couple, these friendly rivals. At bridge,
either Muriel or Coco could be called on for a fourth,
but never both at the same table. Yet, strangely, like all people
so curiously needful, they were the best of friends.

A bowl of roses, a solitary dinner, this is all Conrad wished for in life.
It wasn't his drinking that people didn't like, it was his personality
when he drank. The hell with them. To hell all the stupid
residents of the Sunshine Villas. He'd buy, cook, and eat at his
own pace. He appeared to be a benign, tall, slightly stooped,
gentle-hearted man, and, although their affections were not
returned, most women loved Conrad. Each woman seemed
to find something about themselves they liked in "Connie."
He'd give a waiter a two-dollar tip, even before dining,
and tell "how well" the Help picked up the dishes. How lovely
he could be, thought the occasional woman companion.
There was no solicitude, in turn, toward the women from Conrad
for he rather disliked the lot but could hardly bring himself
to tell them so. He just got nicer and nicer. Thus Conrad
was looked for at every Sunshine Party and, hot with their wiles,
women waited for him to find them, which he never did.
In this way, a quaint nostalgia grew around the elderly
man about that which is and that which is not, the same quality
perhaps seen differently by each seer.

From the everlasting sleep of human confusion, Muriel
was sure that Conrad loved her. Muriel felt it the moment
she met him. And after Coco left her each day at four, Muriel
would stop by to see if Conrad wanted dinner. He never did—
we already described his eating style, but on this particular day
Muriel outfoxed the Conrad man and brought her favorite dish
with her. She didn't warn him of this cooking triumph.
It was "Tuna Olé" and once she'd won a contest with it,
with two prizes, a trip for two to Mexico (which she never took)
and a blue and yellow casserole dish, hand painted (which she did).
Up to the door she came. Conrad looked and he almost got away
but for his shadow which she must have seen crouched behind
the door. The door flung open (he must remember to buy a lock),
and there she was looking straight at him as if he were the last man
left after the bomb had exploded. He looked shaken.
She beamed as if she were about to set off a wonderful memory
all of her own. "I brought you a surprise."

"Delighted, of course, but much too early to eat," Conrad muttered.
"Oh, I'm on a writing schedule and can stay just a very few hours,
but I thought we could share this." Muriel held the dish out before her,
a sacrifice for his altar. "I'm afraid I can't eat whatever it is you've
prepared. Probably not on my doctor's diet."
"Nonsense. Just your wish to be fashionable and you're failing at it.
You are slim enough and look at yourself (wink), good enough to eat."
With this delicate innuendo, she cried, "Olé!" setting the dish squarely
down. "My ex-husband's favorite." She dabbed her eye a little
with the cooking mitt she carried, unfortunately smearing
a bit of cheese on her upper lid. "Death," she said.
Death, he thought. Not the last humiliation by any means.
"Well, I wish I could ask you to stay, Mary."
"Muriel."
"Of course."
"I will then. Thank you." And down she sat, pluck on the plaid soldier's
sofa, harder than it looked, setting her teeth together,
but coming up smiling, nonetheless.

Doing good in the world was very time consuming and Muriel hoped
the higher authorities would take note, maybe God would even
hasten her own writing when an arid place was struck.
Maybe Muriel would be rewarded in this way for her good works.
Coco wrote daily. Coco had but one page finished, but
she claimed perfectionism, and how could one argue against that?
Muriel's own writing, Muriel believed, would come in time.
She had experiences. Perhaps it would come from the same
motivation she had in writing recipes: the wish to nourish, to feed,
to weave together tastes and smells. Yes, that was it. And maybe
she could find a way to bring in a scene about the Indians
of Central California she'd read about. It's true that her own
life had nothing to do with them, but why not expand and bring
in historical context to what one thought. Most writers made things
up about Indians, she was sure. Undaunted (she'd never been west),
Muriel was lighted with the idea of writing an illustrious set of memories
rather than presenting a mundane life chronicle. The Barbizon Plaza
was limited in scope, this she now knew, and its interest appealed only
to the monied, the nostalgic and the enlightened. Granted, it'd be a gift
to the world, but one must consider the market, not like Coco up there,
probably writing and rewriting an image into plainness. Scope! Reach!
That's what was needed in one's autobiography. An Indian connection
might add ginger to the situation. What might Coco be doing?
If she could only take a peek at Coco's memoirs. Just for a second.
A vertical climb on the trellis was not impossible at all.

There was so much Coco wanted to know about Conrad, so much lay behind his sparkling eyes. People with bloodshot eyes were obviously thinkers and readers. She knew if anyone could get him to talk, it would be she. She had a way with people. In high school they had termed her Coquette as an endearment. Conrad (should she call him Connie?) was such a mystery, kept to himself so. Did he like to dine alone, or were the Dining Room hours inconvenient for him? There were so many questions one could pose: does he like tuna? And what exactly happened on the night of October 3, just one week ago from which Muriel was still "recovering." Oh yes, a reporter's job was exactly what Coco felt qualified for. It would take her mind off her memoirs for a moment. The journey inward, so tedious. This would exchange the poetic life for one of analysis and discovery. Self-revelation could wait until later. Facts in the service of truth were Coco's mission for now. She chose a severe blue jacket to wear over her mumu. A yellow lined notepad was thrust in her pocket, and she was ready to begin.

On this fine fall day, Conrad was planting some bulbs in his front garden patch when Coco appeared around the bend, her upper garment contrasting unhappily with her dress. It was the first sight which warned Conrad that this woman whose unfortunate personality (he avoided with rigor) was focused on him. She charged forward, lurching with purpose. He stood and hastily moved to the door. Gossipy women were not for him and besides . . .

"Now, now, Conrad, don't go in quite yet. I'm coming to get you."
He blinked innocently as if to inquire who she could possibly be.
Now he remembered something else about this woman.
She seemed to be always pointing at someone or other.
Now the finger was honing on him.
Coco waggled her finger. "I fancied you'd be out on a bright autumn day like this one. And I want the moment of your time, if you don't mind. We're going to have a moment of autobiography."
Conrad felt confused. He was hoping she had meant hers.
"Yours."
Relief, then panic. "I have none, Miss."
"Don't be coy with me, young man. You know full and well my name is Coco. For we met the day I brought the petition submitting that milkmen come to our doors, like it used to be. Of course, no good came of that as management has no interest in preserving our heritage. People don't like history. Too busy to appreciate the past.
But the past is a place, oh yes, and one which should be saved."
Conrad smiled and put his trowel deep into the earth, standing up, defiantly. But defiance was of little use.

Coco was shocked indeed and said so while aiding the recumbent Muriel to a nearby chair—so sad how she'd fallen from a trellis pruning flowers—but now she was ready and prepared for an expansive intellectual afternoon. They talked at first about cooking, how it was a mirror of what we know about society at large. Then conversation moved on to the lyricism of pain, broken bones, how one could be waylaid in a devotion to public service, the need to be an apostle to literature if upon the writing path, but the struggle to insure against criticism in order to go on, how unqualified approval was bad for the artist's life. It was a rich tapestry of an afternoon and ended too soon, but finally Coco made indications that she must take her leave. She chose her time before saying, "By the way, Muriel, I don't wish to disturb you with a touch of sanity. I know it's unpleasant for you . . ."

Muriel hated Coco to begin like this and braced herself.

Coco continued, "I have it on firsthand authority that Conrad had no intentions for you on your so-called visit with him. He didn't invite you. He didn't want you. He didn't touch you. And he doesn't remember you." She murmured the last, to soften the blow. How important it was in life to have imagination within hope. Coco then leaned down to kiss Muriel's lacquered crown, patting her there sweetly, and looked back to the conformation of a stricken face—which lingered deliciously in her memory all the way back to her home. To cottage Number One.

Stella wasn't sure she liked the idea of stealing a paper
from Miss Coco's desk if even for an hour. Miss Muriel phrased it
convincingly, to be sure, explaining how she was Coco's secret editor and
was trying to further Coco's career against her friend's will . . .
That Coco was basically shy and modest. This last caused Stella's eyebrows,
already furrowed in confusion, to rise straight up in disbelief.
Muriel continued that "Coco would not want any help, and would indeed
remain in anonymity if allowed." This made Stella all the more uncertain.
This did not sound like the Miss Coco she worked for every week,
who stormed about the villa, and was on the phone, hourly,
scheduling herself for appointments with people who did not return
her calls. Coco was not beckoned by anyone, nor did anyone ever show up.
Yet she persisted in hounding the villagers. Stella thought Coco
was far from shy. The fifty-dollar bill was held crisply in Muriel's fingers,
lacquered nails playing with its corner. This
made Stella believe there must be a good cause at the root of all this.
Think about it. A friend who would spend her own money to help another—
Indeed, on Stella's next day at Miss Coco's, ferreting through
the pile of papers, Stella came up on the single page
entitled "My Memoirs." Could this be it? Stella pondered. Once surfaced,
the thin sheet was carefully placed in the folder provided by Miss Muriel.
Stella's heart beat a trifle fast, but there was that fifty-dollar bill waiting
for the delivery and poor Miss Coco "may live forever in shadows
without some aggressive editorial help," Miss Muriel had said.

Safely at home, Muriel opened the folder. She lay upon the pink chintz chaise and took a deep breath, expectantly, scanning quickly. Ha! Where was the lilt of language here? Declaratives sentences starting with the date of Coco's birth! And here her birthweight and first words. Hmmm. This was somewhat similar to Muriel's wonderful work in the beginning, the heartfelt reminiscence about the color yellow, but one could not be sure, and still could never sue for plagiary because the words weren't in the same order and you cannot copyright an idea. This, Muriel had read in one of the author's journals she had sent to her from England. The British were so much more advanced, so much more cultured. Muriel's heart stopped in mid-sentence. There, in large block print was a jeering line—"DEAR MURIEL, I KNOW AT THIS MOMENT YOU ARE READING THIS AND I HAVE MY TRUE MEMOIRS UNDER LOCK AND KEY FOREVER MORE.
HA.HA. YOUR FRIEND, COCO."

Gotta Go Now

[Goss 183 Publications, 2012]

Nothing in the cicada's song
tells it is
going to die

—Basho

HIV

The Chelsea hotel was the most
exciting place I'd ever been—
where artists in the grand
tradition had always lived and worked,
high arched ceilings, marbled mantels,
I, anxious to meet my friend, ordered,
"Take me, taxi,"—this—"to the Chelsea."
This was it. New York City. So
Greg had finally made it.
Visiting was like our casual talks
in Houston; he'd made an apple pie,
unwrapped my book, inscribed to him,
touched and kissed the cover. 1984.
Downstairs is where his lover lived, a
slim and gentle Japanese, critics called
a genius, the loveliest man
you'll ever meet, moving like an angel
across the room to point to paintings
standing free, large as his entire
wall, canvases of angles, pale pure
yellow spheres barely there, creamy lemon
moving through a distant light, transparence
stirred with breath so slight
the drifting images melted swimmingly,
and then within the month it takes for
oil paint to dry, they were all gone.

A Trip Through the 20TH Century with Ann Darr

Hello says the bookshelf
                where Ann lost Ken's book *Amelia Earhart*

Hello says the steamed asparagus
                where Ann forgot the water

Hello says Shakespeare as we sat bone to bone
                at *Midsummer Night's Dream*

Hello says the fake crabmeat salad
                we thought was real

It's all that we wanted
                where nothing was foreign
                each day disguised as an offering

Goodbye St. Mary's dorm rooms
                where we made Ann's books together
                photos of her the aviatrix on top

Goodbye to a tour de force
                of inspiration
                creative output unfolding

Goodbye to things we cannot help
                memory gone but praise and faith
                keeping its promise

Goodbye lone figure on the stage
                radiant angry exuberant
                whitened by moonlight.

In the Attic

for Hilary Tham

 I am writing here. Hilary is correcting my poem.
(I liked it the way it was, vivid with reds and yellows.)
"Too bright,"
she says, retreating back into the shadows.
I begin again. This time I describe the plain pine box
they buried her in.
She sweeps a blue scarf over my eyes,
the color of bluebirds on Chinese New Year.
Hilary wants only the truth from this poem,
and I—so lost—
cannot find it. She shows me
brown chocolates from Florence,
a gray silk shawl from Rome,
a well in Lucca where a young girl drowned in despair.
She holds image after image, reaching out to me.
I am crying while I write.
She smiles. "Find the truth. Your breath is like snow
on the page."
Now I go to the orange trees transplanted
across the river Huai, the river of death
where it is said the same fruit thrives on both sides.
"Go on," she says.
I talk about my husband, the sketchbook she gave him
when he could no longer sculpt,
my daughters she put in her poems.
She smiles. We are getting closer.
I come up with just one line from the Bible,
"How beautiful upon the mountains are the feet of the
messenger announcing the green of memory."
She thinks I'm ready to begin.

Big Mama Thornton

Last time I saw her
she wasn't so big. Actually
she was downright skinny,
singing the final time
in Washington, D.C.

Backstage she drank a
quart of milk
mixed equal parts with
gin—
Seagrams, she told me.

Then she got the idea.
Could I contact the Seagrams
people and then she could
advertise for them and
they'd like her for
drinking a full quart a day—their gin.

I said no, I didn't
think so, and I didn't
think the milk people
would like the commercial so much
either. She still felt bad

about Elvis stealing "Hound Dog,"
the way he did, even though
she was much too much of a lady to say so.
Once she talked about it, long ago,
before she started milk with gin.

I guess the drink left a
sweet taste in her mouth.

With

[Somondoco Press, 2016]

Even when I forget you
I go on looking for you
I believe I would know you
Sometime long ago but then
Other times I am sure you
Were here a moment before
And the air is still alive
Around where you were.

—W.S. Merwin

Gray's Tea Room (1940)

I don't know why they called it a Tea Room.
They didn't serve tea.
In fact I don't know of anything
they served except hot roast beef sandwiches
on Saturday night, with mashed potatoes, 35 cents.
Sometimes my father ordered pork. We sat
on high stools at a counter, and no one thought
to sit on chairs, any more than we expected
a chocolate cake more than once a week
from Fiestal's grocery.

Across the street from Gray's on the corner
was a record store,
and once I asked my father for $5.00
to buy an album of Carmen Cavallaro
playing on the piano.
I couldn't believe my good luck.
He gave it to me just like that,
as if he had another one in his pocket,
and maybe even more.

We felt prosperous at the counter
waiting to be handed dishes
piled high with gravy for people like us
who could order whatever if they want, either beef or pork.

Recently in a classroom, my students argued
whether it were better to have more or enough
and what those two words meant—satisfaction,
expansion, possibilities, ambition—
If philosophically we must have enough
before we can have more,
for more can never come from lack.

For six years I passed Gray's on my way to school
and never thought anyone else was there

or that anything else was ever eaten but what we had.
Gray's was to come alive and open, once a month
on Saturday.

Now when I see a tearoom,
I want to tell them what they're missing,
what with their sad tea and biscuits.
Sometimes, in the late afternoon,
I wish we were all alive, and back on Stuyvesant Avenue.
I like to think of that, when we didn't know
differently, when there was always more than enough.

Three O'Clock (1942)

Elaine's father was a guard at the Trenton State Penitentiary.
Once in awhile, I forget how often,
she couldn't come out to play
because it was her daddy's turn to pull the switch,
and watch a prisoner die.
He'd stay inside feeling sick, but why the family
had to close the shades, I don't know, or
why, even if we knocked politely, her mother
sent us away, saying, "Elaine can't come out to play today."
The rest of us girls sat on my porch
in cool dresses. Three o'clock.
Mothers were in the kitchen setting spoons.
There were iced drinks and cookies,
powdered sugar, a confection of air;
not even fathers were coming home to break the silence.
The only sound is a boy on the tracks
who has caught a small animal and tramps through the weeds
carrying a cardboard cage, three holes for air.
The girls ask whose turn it is to make up a story.
We visit bright imagined countries and
in this way travel beyond swinging chairs,
white railings, a summer porch.
At three o'clock God mutes the trees
to listen. The only sound is a thrashing—
the biting and scratching as the boy falls—
the wrestling and scrambling
of a small animal breaking free.

Tripe

My Aunt Mamie bought it in the Italian store,
A block of paper-mâché-meat, wavy too,
Then she wanted on the board and got the weapons out.
Here's to the art of disintegration,
She starts with this,
The flesh dismembered from its skin,
A knife cut down horizontal lines,
Leaving strips of weeping meat.
"The lining of a cow's stomach,"
My father said, with bright anticipation.
"Florence is famous for this,"
From the city of saints and golden domes,
This wiggling mass, now,
Laid in disarray, pieces
Splayed across the table,
Scored three times across
With blades, sharp, and then salt,
Rubbed onto flesh,
From outside she brought in herbs,
Torn from limb, ripped from earth, lay
Broken by their branches, near the vine,
In this way she made an odd and pleasured
Ritual from what was lost or killed,
To feed our leisured meal,
And slowly in the pot, tomatoes,
Cut and slipped of time,
The stuff moved to steam, sublime,
Flavor somehow like all else saved
By change to change again, better than it was
Before its end, mutilated images
Streaming together now. Cooked five hours.
TRIPE.

Beauty From the World

I miss them,
the Saints,
the ones with masks of pocked faces,
clumps of burned skin,
skin removed so roses could grow
at the throat.
How I knelt to worship their flights
from this physical world, with
flesh turned to light.

Why did History march through with
its rough steps causing a fray of
stories from Lombardy, the Barbarians
storming the castles,
sheep slaughtered in sacrifice.

So we're now told
Saints were invented simply to signal fear
in those savage heathens,
to control their headwinds of power.

Dear Saints, my beautiful haloed statues,
were you created merely to trim a booth at Christ's Fair?
Remember all those altars with flowers in my room?
Our thriving practice of worship together?

Have you left me from the high pantheon of faith
to this lonely kingdom of words?

Cottage Cheese

I couldn't believe my eyes
at the YWCA Cafeteria
on Spring Street
right behind Dunham's
Department Store where I
sold and modeled teenage clothing
every day after school.
Cottage cheese on a pear on a
lettuce leaf, I'd never seen
such a thing before. In my
house—ricotta, yes, fruit, yes, salad,
but here it was—so fancy,
so superior, half a pear
from a can somewhere,
maybe Wisconsin or wherever
genuine canned things came from.
It was right next to the danish
behind a glass wall. I watched the
stream of people walking past
to the automat
to get coffee at the end
but there'd be nothing better
for me to buy if Heaven and Hell met that
day at the YWCA on Spring Street.
One dollar for the dish. Cottage cheese
on a pear. I was free. I was American.
I was there.

Harbinger

You'll never get it finished
Don't even try
You can never return a life payment of kindness and hurt
You'll never arouse your first love again
You'll never learn the geography of the archipelago or name
Those yellow flowers shaped like angels by the side of the road
And you don't care anymore about who bought you the white straw hat
You'll never visit the snow in Russia
Or play chess
Or service a computer
Forget it
Not in this lifetime
Your skin will never be soft and pink as your first child's
Nothing is left
So just be good
Don't try to be good
BE good
How? Don't ask
Just do it
The rest is none of your business.

Lunatics

Rivers like veins   taken by night
By what we remembered   now dry
Leaving their shadows   leaving our shadows
Behind   a big achievement for the sun
Which will be remembered   for our failures
Once the Anglicized air was sweet and pure
Now a scar   on our cheeks   of smoke
Touch it   we are the lunatics   who
Slept   with moonlight   on our   faces
Legend says   that   makes you crazy
And indeed   dry land   dead water   we
Must have been.

Release

Forget what I said before—
It's evening in Tuscany.

Someone is making bread that will not grow stale,
others are picking *carciofi*.

The moon won't speak one word,
so covered with the moss of clouds.

I know someone who died, but stays.
I would live it all again.

Nothing is divested but the
crêpe myrtle that screams pink.

Nothing is enough but the
empty wastebasket where letters once were.

Hat of Snow

Your sadness is not a blizzard   of shrapnel made of metal
that cuts and bleeds and kills.   It's just a snowstorm
                    that passes and melts.

Pretend there's ice and   snow on the street
and we can cover it   with white flowers
                    which will never die.

I would tell you to take   some of those flowers
and make a hat   and, for the joy of it
go into the world,   because that too will melt
but you'll have   had   a hat of flowers.
                    How many can say that.

Athena Has Swag

Athena always tells the Truth
And she is afraid of nothing
She does not know any better
That's the good thing about being mythological

She does not encounter or counter
She is very smart and says
No one ever solved a problem by being dumb
Everyone forgets her but B+ students

Athena was not what they expected
Tilting into the back story of Greece
But if parallels must be drawn then lift her out of sleep
Bring her back in four-inch heels

And purple fingernails
Put her in my body
I'm not afraid to be forgotten
She needed everyone who ever died

To give her new feelings to feel
So I do but please
Do not attack her because she wins at archery
And let us forgive her for still wanting romance—

Esther Phillips

(Blues singer once known as "Little Esther")

After clinging so hard to the side of the ship
Along the edge
There was only water beneath
The steep hill climbed made hard with feet
After the snow in hot places
Distant and hungry
The blood you shared not mythical but actual
Not at this late state little Esther not now when
You sang "What a Difference a Day Makes"
Don't go back now where there's no music
Your face is in your hands like used soil
Sing it out again
You're almost home
Don't take that sick stuff *no more*
Chase those devils back. Don't leave us. Not after all this.

Alternate Theories

In answering my husband, I said, "I only
wonder about ideas I can use in

poetry." He said this may be a waste
of wonder. Yes. I realize it's not a fair

market exchange, rationing my thoughts
this way. Here we were walking

in the woods—noticing fern. He said
he could make green herbs grow all

winter long in the kitchen—
the white receptacle by the window,

the constancy of a blue
Glo-light—the waters of life

dripped in every day with care.
I said, "I'd like that. It's lighted

up until morning. Like the moon."
Finally something I can use,

helpful to me—while writing in the dark—
for nothing can be seen exactly as we describe it.

Summoning the Moment

The importance of saying this now
is that it can't be said later.

By then we won't remember seeing
the crow in the trail of his cousins,

or remember that, just like us,
he has more intelligence than he needs

for survival.
We won't recall that

something unseen exists beyond
flights into pillars of clouds, and skies of fire.

Suppose you are on your death bed,
will you know all the

names for Love?
We won't remember, then, seeing the blaze

of sounds, towards silence,
when stepping out of this movie

into the ever-expanding
transcendence.

We can write
as if there's no eternity.

This simple narrative, engraved, is all we have,
if truthfully said.

Even birds know that to sing their song
is to summon the moment before flying.

Vanishing Reflections

Memory is one way the world rids itself of us.
     How she was in the beginning . . .
When we move forward, I tell her,
something will always be left back.
That's the way it always is with the girl.
     The girl: what is it she wants to tell me?
Beneath the pier, its planks washed by salt air, she sits,
waiting for her salvation, waiting for my writing.

     If I can find the problem to solve,
the puzzle, the argument, I can replace her sorrow
with a brilliant diffusion/illusion of who she is.

     Look at her wanting me to write
about an apple. And then her eating it instead. What can
possibly happen, with such behavior?

     Writing is about consequence, I tell her,
and she is like the wind
     pitching in all directions. Now there she goes
walking through the dead grasses high as her waist.
     Now she dissolves into her own reflection.

     Persistence with the past negotiates her life,
sometimes she wants to write
     a single word for dream again and again,
papered over with her emotions.
     I am not sentimental
but she stains everything she touches with tears.

     She says she will haunt me until I *feel* something.
I say I will not be stalked by a dream guided by her imaginings.

Her allure is something that cannot be caught,
things invisible only the Seer can see.
     Now she is under the apple tree.
Now she's the bird in the tree,

now the feathers.
If you believe in something enough,
time's sweet crawl will bring her back.
        She comes only so she can leave.
        She comes for that.

The Man Who Got Away

[New Academia/Scarith Press, 2014]

I have thee not / but yet I see thee still—

—Hamlet

1952

There you sit in the open cockpit
I never saw such a smile
Goggles pushed up on your head
Shoulders harnessed with a parachute
To keep you safe
This would be before you were on nine carriers
Before exile to Viet Nam
Before your children surrounded you like stars
Waiting for your kiss
Before the autumns of our lives
Before there would be no autumns
Before I said don't fly away
Before you would become someone else
Then back again
Before there would be so much sun outside without you
Before the winds were light and variable
Before you'd sit on the front step every time
I went to the store waiting for my return
There you are sitting in a cockpit of an SNJ
Smiling at me for all eternity
In a moment that could not last
Cleared for flight
Everything in the whole blue world
Ahead of you.

I'll Take That As a Compliment

Dancing in the basement of the Pentagon
every Friday night—they'd open up for
disco lessons and how we'd been waiting
to learn those steps. Elaine, the accountant in
my office, would come with her new boyfriend
although his little kids vomited on her
their first time at the picnic,
but maybe they could make it after all to
this kind of carefree bouncing fast music.
Her husband locked her out and kept the
family punch bowl, and Ken and I were badly
in need to find something new in our marriage.
This just might be it, finding the moves to
Donna Summer urging us on. Oh yes, they
pushed the desks aside to clear the space
for continuing education in the Pentagon
basement for people like us, except the
only trouble is we both wanted to lead. We
learned the grapevine and the sidewind and
outlasted Elaine and Ted, but every week
we found we needed to start all over again.
Maybe if we had a strobe light, my husband
said. I'm willing to. Are you?

Glass Metal Salt

for Ken in intubaton

Your hands once on my neck so transparent
I could see through them in my sleep,
as I move into the city of windows lying at my feet,
I am in the third dimension
on a flat map world—

My monk in the machine! Talk to me. Anything,
tell me how it breathes for you, pumping
against your will. Tell me how you love heavy metal,
my pilot, my race car driver, my sculptor,
how you want to get your hands on it, make it move,

fly, shape and burnish it. I see you know—it's winning—
This is the one thing you cannot bend, but if I know you,
and I do—you'll die trying for command.
What am I now? A chess piece on a flat glass floor, breaking beneath
my feet. A note in a bottle uncorked, unread,

unless you'll rip the tubes out, breathe on your own, before
I leave to turn back one last time.
Please call out to me. Say something. Tell me who I am now.
Even Lot's wife must have had a name before
they called her Salt.

Stunned

I don't know about dropping a full bottle of wine on the pavement in Pisa
Or both leaving our hats in the locker room in Maryland on the same day
Or talking about our neighbor in West Virginia who killed his cat
As we stand hand in hand looking
At the milk of the moon shining on the whole world
I alive—you dead—saying if this could happen, anything could.

Can I Count on You

If I were lying in a boat in a wedding gown would you see me floating by
If I named a star after you would you lie in the grass looking up
If I lived in a white house would you come sit on my front porch
If I were caught in a bad dream would you please wake me up
If I had a plaid blouse would you help me button it
If I could jitterbug would you do the double dip
If I were a red cardinal would you hold out a sunflower seed
If I caught all the fireflies in the world would you give me a big jar
If the night nurse forgets to come would you bring me a glass of water
If I have only minutes to look at the silky moon will you come get me

One Year Ago Today

January, 2014

You came into the kitchen and I was making tea—and you said
I feel a little debilitated today
You wore your warm gray sweatshirt
but your hands were shaking
and you said
I'll just take some cough medicine and go on back to bed
This was hours before the ambulance

Today, one year later, I felt a little debilitated myself
So I took some cough medicine and went back to bed
and dreamed you wanted to come Christmas shopping
You wanted to come with me to get yourself a gift
a science kit for sculpting
as yours was empty
I had one bag left that we could use

I took my floppy hat and biked down the hill
and stopped to call you at McDonalds
but my phone was home with you
The nice young girl let me use hers but you didn't answer
so up the hill I went to tell you where we'd meet
And you were there!   You were here!

In your bright red sweater in my office in my chair
Today   Of all days
You always said that you knew how to thrill me
and you do   you do   you were there.

Looking at the Sight of His Back

We rise to tea and homemade bread,
talk of a friend and read a prayer,
go swimming, nap, take a
machine to the fixer, cook pasta
in clam sauce, we drink vodka
martinis, how we complain about
our last house guest, we light a fire
in the fireplace, eat dinner,
read a book, the day
slips beneath our surface,
how long were the shadows
tucked into the sly folds of our
marriage, we kept looking at the
sky trying to make sense of it,
no one else could do that for us,
those who loved us and left
no longer mattered, if we stop telling this story
it will go away.

Learning from Buddha

The cat likes to lick
a piece of butter
at the end of a knife
propped up by the window
so he can watch the birds
today I forgot the butter and the knife
he didn't care
he knows
some days
there are no birds.

Other Voices Other Lives

[Alan Squire Publishing, 2018]

Pierced by a sudden joy . . .
—T.S. Eliot

How a Poem Begins

It's a little thing. Could be
the long *o*'s in Kosovo, or
a woman
alone in the street
after the hurricane
sweeping Honduras.
Perhaps we tell of a child
beneath the flood
in New Orleans, or
feet bloody from
walking the rubble
of Afghanistan.
They say poetry is
insignificant,
such a tiny voice
no one can hear.
Sometimes it says
"I can't breathe."
That's why we write of such
little things, insignificant
things.

Identification

Upstairs on Warren Street, in the jewelry shop, we watched
the jeweler carve the letters of our names
with all the dollars that you'd saved.

It was silver with my name on the front in cursive swirls,
and yours, BLOCK letters on the back.
I was seventeen and we wore matching figured sweaters, the style then,
blue with white stars, woolen, like sweaters at that time.

Years passed, houses and children came and went and
I forgot the time and money that we spent
                    until you died
and then, among your "Personals"—dog tags, worn to Laos
(although you thought it would be just another cruise)—there,
attached to your dog tags, my I.D. bracelet fixed chain to chain,
to bring you safely home again.

I put it around my wrist and wore it every day these past two years
until it went away last week. Where it dropped, I'll never
know. I searched every store and drawer, dove down the
swimming pool to reach the bottom. Others helped. I called

each place I'd been and then dear Cindy bought
a brand new one which I'll engrave with our old names,
but now I know the sign—I think—
You, Ken, carried it to sea and now took it back again,

generous Indian giver, saying "I release you now to start life,
a new life, to start again, unchained—
Your old identification with me is gone—You are saying:
"You, My Darling Wife," in silver scroll, "are free."

Mechanical Physics

I never knew how to put two pieces together—
Say, the garden hose, for example, its nozzle undetectable.
I flooded the new coffee pot because the sections didn't quite match.
Can you imagine how hard it was to convince myself I could do anything

With more than one panel—I didn't even try.
IKEA sent furniture in boxes, all marked # 44.
I could feel the lessons yet to learn, the escape from reason, I could feel
my human failure before UPS left the house.

Now in the lightness of the last of this day,
how do I know who will hold me at sunset?
I cannot make the alive and the dead parts come together, as we once were.
I cannot match the seams—square the ending.

Safety

for Ken Flynn

When you were in the ninth grade and I was in the seventh, you were
a crossing guard keeping order at Junior High School Number 3. No one
was disobedient when you wore that wide yellow strap across your chest—
no one bruised another, caused trouble, or so much as threw a stone—
no one cracked a joke about you, a man in uniform. How did
that yellow vest feed your soul to let you know someday you'd
fly a plane just to feel the power of a strap across your chest. What
liberation—to know how to be in charge—strong and capable—
flying through gunfire and lightning again and again to come back to me.
Although we were young, you were fifteen and I was thirteen, since then,
I've never known the world without you. Now I must be twelve.

Everything Is Smaller Than the Truth

Knowing the worst, he is gone,
I still try to learn the way of sleep

while the night pressing down on me
holds its basket of dreams

out of reach. I have
taken loss into account, yet

the border of my skin grows thin
with the white of sheet and the

slivers of light under the door,
tying my wish to the moon.

It does no good,
the canopy of thought is darker,

is stronger than
prayer keeping time to the beat of my heart,

now it is dawn. What language is this
with its different group of birds

telling me the day, its terrible truth,
is going on before me.

Locator

I don't know why love works. Yet it's
undeniable, every line of it hand-tooled

like a finely wrought page.
This is very exciting, the extra beat that my

heart skipped, because marriage is discipline
like an athlete's, with the grace of a dance.

It is stillness and silence, the
end of our differences.

Surely our bodies were always
prepared for it. I was on the

verge of sorrow when I thought of this,
this tissue, this sustaining

legend: here's the door
that will not close. The outcome is uncertain.

Why do you torture me for explanations?
I only know love is the bed of gold we lie on.

Work Is My Secret Lover

Jazzmen even refer to sex as work.
Some primitive people believe
That death is
                    —Paul Zimmer

Work
takes the palm of my hand to kiss
in the middle of the night
It holds my wrist lightly and feels the pulse
Work is who you find with me
when you tiptoe up the stairs
and hear my footsteps through the shadows
You'll see me lift my arm
to stretch and then lean down
to put my head to it
Work threatened to die once
for all that was left unsaid
so I took to it like a young bride
flushed with excitement
adultery too yes I admit it
On all the holidays
when others gathered at the table I was dreaming of it
making love to the movement of paper
the words for my lips
the feel of it
Sometimes when company came
I'd throw a tablecloth over my Work and set the plates and
everyone acted as if nothing were visible
pretending I was the good hostess that I was
While on the Christmas tree Work waited patiently
among ornaments gleaming like a groom
I am guilty as charged
for nothing else could buy my feelings
and why would I sell the only thing that ever loved me the way
I loved back
but my beautiful long-lasting
faithful lover my friend who will never leave.

What the Psychic Said

[Goss183 Publications, 2021]

He made the storm to be still
and the waves of the sea were hushed

(P107:28-29)

Athena Sees

the sleeping sun slipping away

as if it had another day

yet how good and true the light is

how it never lets us down

showing up again and again

from its sunny dream

every single day from every single night

like a basket of happiness

fair to everyone rich and poor alike

and how much how much you can love

the sky because it will always be there.

Just This

The Buddha

The water to the left turning

then to the right past barbed fences

leaning past trees once again alive

up then down the valley you like

what you see spring summer

it doesn't matter to walk by the water

is to see white seasons turning green to blue

swarms of flying sparks with wings in the

closing darkness then morning comes

past your sight verging so we want to close

our eyes then to open to find some meaning

find purpose for movement and we slow down

then we find there is no meaning but motion.

Just this. Again. Just this.

The Tribe

of soaring strangers, the curious, the blooming—
Joseph Brodsky in a labor camp   for writing the people's language,
Adrienne Rich: "Take ourselves more seriously /
. . . a deeper listening cleansed of oratory, formulas . . ."
I thank them for the future—
The double narratives of Louise Gluck's words   spacious and small for
memory not yet imagined   of children separated at the border.
The real   the will   commitment   Rita's "Thomas and Beulah" bringing to life
more than a muse could create.
You ask about resistance and how we can keep going   I say:
Blake's revolutionary "Meet on the coast / glowing with blood,"
words rinsed from a corrupt court.   Patricia Smith: "All my fists at once?"
Espada with "Music and Spanish rose before the bread . . ./Praise and bread."
We praise the bread of those who are our tribe and where we are strong,
where we belong. Alexie, "Everyone is a half-breed," even those on either side
of the fence   where   language flies across   like unchained birds.

May Day

He said they gave him
a white "Flash" suit—
like outer spacemen wear.
They said, "Put it on and
get into your cockpit."

What peril this was
he did not know
until they praised his plane
that held "your atom bomb."

A trail of thoughts
across his mind—
a sweep of stars beyond—
his children—their children.
his house—their house.

Pale with sadness
and hate, he knew what
he would do.

Ditch the plane in water!
the deepest part—
the bomb would dwell inert
and he would raft home from
the Turkish seas.

He was a calm man,
a survival expert—
he figured it out—
It would take
maybe four months.

His heart was a meteor
exploding in his children's
backyard under the apple tree—

It dazzled the swing set,
the rowboat filled
with toys and sand—

his wife in a pink and white
sundress
looking up at the sky.

The Lady Reads My Palm

It's not luck you need to read the stars. It's the
shape of sorrow in your cup.
You once saw the wild ground
turn to shells beneath your feet.
You saw the gorgeous salt of the ocean
turning blue. You walked on melting sand and
now the lonely fervor quiets.
Take your marriage off the shelf. Dust it.
Make sense of this love where rock becomes air.
Who will sit with you.
Who will read your poems.
Please take back your ring.
It's worth more than paper, gold or cash.
There's a song inside your finger
saying more than a letter.
Take love.
Hold it to your ear and you will see a vision.
The shepherd moves across the fields.
You'll hear a name calling you home.

Let's Not Shoot the Poets

They fish at night
and dig by day
They were not born for death
their heavens are low enough to touch
flashing illumination and desire

They make spring beautiful
They listen in their heads
for autumn's breaking
They create and work
turning deadwood to life

Society's not enough
so they fly above
its deception and
crash into clouds of meaning
The bucolic would not
exist but for their masterpiece

Hostile fire, stay
away from the crush
of boats crowding
the shore—filled
with possible poets—

They are like animals
birthing but never forgetting
their loss   Poems
may be crushed but memory
is the hot gold made every day
they stay

Athena's Dirty Little Secret

I opened the windows of clouds from a high tower
and saw   as the goddess of power   caught as I am in midair
that the green stands still on earth   the geese are clucking
I saw the empty shoes from children   left beside the stair
I saw them coming   up the hill toward me
I saw that this is what I wanted all along   the children
to pour milk   to open the door   I wanted to be there.

This Poem Is Asking for Your Love

This poem is not usually like this
I don't know what came over it
It's mostly violet under the sun
with a large yellow parasol and a pond
with a center that never freezes
I swear I had no idea
I'm so used to trees of hearts and
cherries within its branches
I can't imagine
what woke this poem up
with a truth I never wanted
It called out the tower window and said
I was alone
That in itself is a morbid lie
I have long shadows in autumn and clouds
anytime there is a sky
In fact everything was going so well until
this poem wanted to undress me
and bring back my love
and hold me close and rub
my forehead when I had fever
It had no idea what trouble could come
from this so I wrote it
then I ran from it
now I can erase it
to show I never needed it after all
because don't you know, Poem,
if you have to ask for something
it's no gift.

About the Author

Grace Cavalieri is Maryland's tenth Poet Laureate. Her new books are *Grace Art: Poems & Paintings* and *The Secret Letters of Madame de Stael* (both 2021). She founded and produces "The Poet and the Poem" for public radio, now from the Library of Congress, celebrating 47 years on air. This series of interviews with poets was shot to the moon in the Lunar Codex in 2022 as the first podcast series on the moon. Among other awards she holds the Corporation for Public Broadcasting's Silver Medal and the George Garrett Award for Outstanding Community Service in Literature from AWP.

Other Books by Grace Cavalieri
(Not included in this collection)

Why I Cannot Take a Lover (Washington Writers' Publishing House, 1975)
Body Fluids (The Bunny and the Crocodile Press, 1976)
Greatest Hits (Pudding House Press, 2002)
What I Would Do for Love (Jacaranda Press, 2004)
    (Italian Translation: Forest Woods Media, 2013)
Water on the Sun (Bordighera Press, 2006)
The Mandate of Heaven (Bordighera Press, 2014)
Life Upon the Wicked Stage (New Academia/Scarith Press, 2015)
Showboat (Goss183, 2019)
The Secret Letters of Madame de Stael (Goss183, 2021)
Grace Art: Poems & Paintings (Poets Choice Publishing, 2021)
Four Plays by Grace Cavalieri Including "Anna Nicole: Blonde Glory"
    (Forest Woods Media Productions, 2023)

About The Word Works

Since its founding in 1974, The Word Works has steadily published volumes of contemporary poetry and presented public programs. Its imprints include The Washington Prize, The Tenth Gate Prize, The Hilary Tham Capital Collection, and International Editions.

Monthly, The Word Works offers free programs in its Café Muse Literary Salon. Starting in 2023, the winners of the Jacklyn Potter Young Poets Competition will be presented in the June Café Muse program.

As a 501(c)3 organization, The Word Works has received awards from the National Endowment for the Arts, the National Endowment for the Humanities, the D.C. Commission on the Arts & Humanities, the Witter Bynner Foundation, Poets & Writers, The Writer's Center, Bell Atlantic, the David G. Taft Foundation, and others, including many generous private patrons.

An archive of artistic and administrative materials in the Washington Writing Archive is housed in the George Washington University Gelman Library. The Word Works is a member of the Community of Literary Magazines and Presses and its books are distributed by Small Press Distribution.

wordworksbooks.org

Other New & Selected Collections from The Word Works:

Barbara Goldberg: *Breaking & Entering: New and Selected Poems*
Michael Klein: *The Early Minutes of Without: Poems Selected & New*
Judith McCombs: *The Habit of Fire: Poems Selected & New*

Printed in the USA
CPSIA information can be obtained
at www.ICGtesting.com
LVHW090115291023
762449LV00005B/1029